S0-ACV-368

The Rapture

A Question of Timing

William R. Kimball

BAKER BOOK HOUSE

Grand Rapids, Michigan 49506

Copyright © 1985
College Press Publishing Company
Reprinted 1985 by Baker Book House
with permission of copyright owner

Printed and bound in the
United States of America
All Rights Reserved

Library of Congress Catalog Card Number: 85-71275
International Standard Book Number: 0-8010-5468-0

This book is dedicated to
Terry Edwards and Francis Anfuso,
steadfast friends and
"fellowlabourers, whose names are
in the Book of Life."
Philippians 4:3

Contents

Index of Terms

The following Index has been included to assist the reader in comprehending some of the more common prophetic terms found within this book. This list represents only a general definition of the terms used. There are usually a variety of conflicting viewpoints within the context of each term.

1. *Rapture* - This is a term which is applied to the scriptural event characterizing the translation of the living saints and the resurrection of the dead saints to meet Christ in the air when He returns.

2. *Premillennialist* - A person who believes that Christ will return for the church before He establishes His millennial reign of one thousand years upon the earth.

3. *Amillennialist* - Generally speaking, a person who does not believe in a literal millennial reign of Christ upon the earth after His second coming, or a one thousand year period of world wide peace and righteousness before the end of this present world order.

4. *Postmillennialist* - Generally speaking, a person who does not believe in a literal millennial reign of Christ upon the earth after His second coming. Instead, they see the kingdom of God being victoriously extended in the present world through the preaching of the gospel. They believe that the world will be eventually Christianized prior to Christ's return. They generally spiritualize the millennium and apply it to the church age.

5. *Pretribulationism* - A belief which teaches that Christ will come to remove the church from the earth prior to a final period of great tribulation.

6. *Posttribulationism* - A belief which teaches that Christ will come for the church at the conclusion of a final period of tribulation, and that the rapture and the second coming are synonymous events.

7. *Dispensationalism* - A teaching which maintains that God has divided time into seven distinct periods in which He deals with humanity according to the unique character and qualifications of a particular period.

8. *Futurism* - Generally speaking, a belief which maintains that major prophetic portions of scripture are yet to be fulfilled in a futuristic setting. This can include such distinctive events as

9

the appearance of antichrist, the great tribulation, and a rebuilt temple in Jerusalem, etc.

9. *Historist* - Generally speaking, a historist views major prophetic portions of scripture such as Revelation against the backdrop of the unfolding drama of the church age rather than isolating them to a strict, futuristic setting.

10. *Eschatology* - The study of final things. Eschatology is a study of prophetic events associated with the end times.

Introduction

One of the most prominent areas of interest on the prophetic calendar of events is the rapture. The rapture is firmly established as a centerpiece in biblical eschatology, for this climactic event represents the "blessed hope" of all true believers. It is not surprising, therefore, that the issue of the church's eventual reunion with Christ continues to play an integral and deserving part in any comprehensive treatment of biblical eschatology.

Though the term "rapture" abounds in prophetic literature, it, like the word "trinity," is never mentioned in the scriptures. It is derived from the Latin word *rapio* which means "to seize or carry away." However, in spite of its complete absence in scriptures, the underlying concept of the "catching up of the saints" captured in this term accurately reflects a genuine prophetic event.

The biblical teaching undergirding the concept of the rapture is referred to in the key proof passages of I Thessalonians 4:15-18 and I Corinthians 15:51-53:

For this we say unto you by the word of the Lord, that we which are alive and remain unto the coming of the Lord shall not prevent them which are asleep. For the Lord himself shall descend from heaven with a shout, with the voice of the archangel, and with the trump of God: and the dead in Christ shall rise first: Then we which are alive and remain shall be caught up together with them in the clouds, to meet the Lord in the air: and so shall we ever be with the Lord. Wherefore comfort one another with these words (I Thess. 4:15-18, KJV).

Behold, I shew you a mystery; We shall not all sleep, but we shall all be changed, In a moment, in the twinkling of an eye, at the last trump: for the trumpet shall sound, and the dead shall be raised incorruptible, and we shall be changed. For this corruptible must put on incorruption, and this mortal must put on immortality (I Cor. 15:51-53).

While all Bible-believing Christians embrace the truths contained within these verses, not all find a common ground of consensus concerning this crucial subject. Widespread controversy continues to surround the fundamental issue of timing. In fact, the scriptural validity of the rapture is not where the basic disagreement lies, but in the question of the timing when this event will occur. Herein is the crux of the problem. The question of timing is at the very heart of the controversy, and it is around this pivotal issue that much of the ongoing debate revolves.

Generally speaking, Christians are divided into two basic schools of disagreement. They either believe that the rapture will be a secret, silent event which will occur just before a final period of end-time turbulence known as The Great Tribulation, or that it will occur immediately after this apocalyptic period of turmoil and is synonymous with the visible, public return of Christ in judgment and glory.

Though, historically, Christians have enthusiastically embraced the biblical doctrine of Christ's second coming, a significant cross-section of contemporary Christians see another "coming" before Christ's final return in judgment. They contend that Christ will return to mysteriously evacuate the church before the unprecedented terrors of The Great Tribulation engulf the planet earth.

Advocates of this position are referred to as "pretribulationists." Pretribulationists can be broken down into three basic categories: 1) Those who teach that the rapture will transpire at the beginning of a seven year tribulation period; 2) The "mid-tribulation" school who base their theory upon their interpretation of Daniel's 70th week prophecy, and maintain that the church will be raptured at the mid-point

12

of the final seven year period; and 3) The "partial rapturist" school which teaches that only a select company of spiritually elite saints will be raptured prior to, or during, a final tribulation period.

Advocates of either the "pretrib," "mid-trib," or "partial rapturist" school separate the rapture from Christ's coming in judgment by several years in time. They divide the second coming into two distinct stages with such statements as, "The second coming of Christ is in two stages. First He comes 'for' the saints, and then later He comes back 'with' the saints"; "The day of Christ is the first stage, and the day of the Lord is the second stage"; and "The rapture is the first stage—when Christ comes back for His church—the second stage is when He returns in judgment." In referring to these "two comings," pretribulationists have coined the phrase "double coming." Others have termed them a "split rapture," while still others speak of "two phases" of the second coming.

Regardless of the subtle shades of differences in pretrib eschatology, each of these schools see another coming of Christ before His visible return in judgment. Each of these divisions are sincerely convinced that the rapture is a separate and distinct event from Christ's public return in glory.

Within recent years, the controversy surrounding the timing of the rapture has intensified. This crucial issue has been repeatedly thrust into the forefront of prophetic debate. An abundant amount of fervor, verbage, and outright sensationalism has often been generated over this volatile area of interest. Numerous authors and lecturers, on both sides of the prophetic fence, have been responsible for bringing the subject of timing into clear focus. Supporters of pretribulationism have been especially prolific in their writings, and vocal in addressing this issue. The result has been that a majority of Christians have fallen in step with the "pied pipers" of pretribulationism. Many have done so unquestioningly, without a personal investigation of scripture. They have simply acquiesced to this popular teaching because of the spiritual caliber of those who defend it, because they have never been taught otherwise, because they are unaware and ill-informed concerning opposing perspectives, or because of the erroneous assumption that pretribulationism is an ancient and honorable doctrine which the church has defended since apostolic times.

However, many Christians are currently involved in a prophetic transformation which cuts across every denominational boundary. An increasing number of Christians are taking a second look at biblical eschatology, and are finding serious scriptural weaknesses in the pretribulational position. The consequence of this prophetic reappraisal has been an increasing defection from the ranks of pretribulationist theology in some sectors of Christendom. This trend appears to be gaining momentum.

Though many are in the process of renouncing the concept of a pretribulation rapture, they are not rejecting the rapture itself. They still hold that it is a valid, scriptural concept. However, they are rejecting the notion that the second coming of Christ is subsequent to the rapture in terms of years. To them, the rapture of the church is equivalent to the one and only second coming of Christ at the end of this present age.

Those who oppose a pretribulational emphasis are referred to as posttribulationists. This simply means that they believe that the rapture will occur after a period of great tribulation, and not before. However, it should be pointed out that not all proponents of posttribulationism believe in a future seven year period of unparalleled distress known as The Great Tribulation. But all posttribulationists find common agreement in the fact that Christ's second coming is synonymous with the translation of the saints. They maintain that when the scriptures speak of the second coming, they are not subtly implying two "stages" or "phases" of His return. They reject the teaching that Christ will come to mysteriously remove His church before a final period of intense tribulation.

Those who believe in a posttribulation rapture contend that pretribulationism is a fairly recent innovation in eschatological teaching and does not accurately reflect the historical position of the church. They further maintain that pretribulationism, in whatever form, is an erroneous assumption based upon a faulty exegesis of scripture, and that the preponderance of scriptural evidence against it is substantial.

In the following chapters, I will offer a thorough examination of the rapture. I will endeavor to do so by carefully considering the major points of controversy between pretribulationists and posttribulationists. We will review the historical origins of pretribulationism and explore the factors, trends, and individuals which influenced its development. We will also interact with a variety of conflicting scriptural perspectives in an attempt to unravel the internal difficulties contained within this difficult subject.

1

The Historic Authenticity
of Pretribulationism

A Marked Absence

The controversy surrounding the concept of a pretribulation rapture can be brought into clearer perspective by tracing its historic origins. When reviewing the historical record of the church we soon discover an amazing fact. Even a casual survey of church history reveals the startling reality that there is little in its eschatological heritage to support pretribulationism or dispensationalism prior to the early 1830's.

For the most part, pretribulationists are reluctant to admit this fact. Though many students of the Bible earnestly maintain that pretribulationism is an ancient and venerable doctrine essential to the Christian faith, they are hard-pressed to provide any substantial, historical proof that this teaching was embraced and defended during the 1800 years of eschatological interpretation prior to the prophetic awakening of the early nineteenth century. Their success in doing so has been lackluster at best.

Even Ironside, a fervent dispensationalist, boasted of the marked absence of dispensationalist teachings (which includes the integral concept of a pretrib rapture) in one of his books entitled, *The Mysteries of God*:

> It is scarcely to be found in a single book or sermon through a period of 1600 years! If any doubt this statement, let them search . . . the remarks of the so-called Fathers, both pre and post Nicene, the theological treatises of the scholastic divines, Roman Catholic writers of all shades of thought, the literature of the Reformation, the sermons and expositions of the Puritans, and the general theological works of the day. He will find the "mystery" conspicuous by its absence.[1]

What an incredibly self-incriminating testimony!

Ironside's comments indicate a prevalent attitude embraced by many. His candid remarks show a flagrant disregard, bordering on open contempt, for the historical position of the church regarding pretribulationism. His quote serves as an open acknowledgment that dispensationalism (a key element of which is a pretrib rapture) is one of comparatively recent origin, and cannot be substantiated by historical evidence prior to the 1830's.

Many scholars can attest to the fact that a pretribulation rapture cannot be found in prophetic writings prior to the early 1830's. For example, Alexander Reese stated that,

> . . . the undeniable fact is that this "any-moment" view of Christ's return only originated about 1830 when Darby gave forth, at the same time, the mistaken theory of the Secret Coming and Rapture; but all down the centuries there had existed Christians who longed for the revelation of Christ, whilst expecting that Antichrist would come first. . . . All down the centuries the church expected Christ's coming after the arrival of Antichrist, according to the teaching of Christ and His apostles. Only in 1830 did a school arise that treats with intolerance, and often with contempt, the attitude of those who had looked for Him in the manner just named. Not the slightest respect was paid to a view that had held the field for 1,800 years.[2]

Cameron concurred:

> Now, be it remembered, that prior to that date, no hint of any approach to such belief can be found in any Christian literature from Polycarp

---

1. H. A. Ironside, *The Mysteries of God*, p. 50.
2. Alexander Reese, *The Approaching Advent of Christ*, p. 227.

down . . . . Surely, a doctrine that finds no exponent or advocate in the whole history and literature of Christendom, for eighteen hundred years after the founding of the church—a doctrine that was never taught by a Father or Doctor of the Church in the past—that has no standard Commentator or Professor of the Greek language in any Theological School until the middle of the nineteenth century, to give it approval, and that is without a friend, even to mention its name amongst the orthodox teachers or the heretical sects of Christendom—such a fatherless and motherless doctrine, when it rises to the front, demanding universal acceptance, ought to undergo careful scrutiny before it is admitted and tabulated as part of "the faith once for all delivered unto the saints."[3]

Another author commented upon the first origins of the two-stage rapture theory as follows:

About a hundred years ago, a man named J. N. Darby founded a group of Christians who have become known as "the Brethren," or "Plymouth Brethren." His followers, Wm. Kelly, W. Trotter, and C. H. M. were pioneers of the movement, but in more recent times, W. E. Blackstone in "Jesus Is Coming," F. W. Grant, James M. Gray, A. C. Gaebelein, F. C. Ohman, and particularly C. I. Scofield, the author of the *Scofield Reference Bible,* have popularized what we may call a new view of the events preceding and following the coming of Christ. It is important to note that there is a vast difference between the teachings of these men and the teachings of the old historic premillennialists.[4]

In spite of these and similar statements, some have tried to establish a credible basis of support for a pretrib rapture. Some, like Blackstone, have argued that the pretribulation rapture teaching did not emerge in the prophetic consciousness until fairly recent times due to the restraining forces of spiritual darkness and ignorance which prevailed during the Dark Ages. However, with the dawn of the Reformation, the "rediscovered truths" of pretribulationism were released from the shackles of obscurity and neglect and once again restored to their rightful place of prominence:

The church, hand and hand with the world, plunges into the Dark Ages, until awakened by the great reformers of the sixteenth century,

---

3. Robert Cameron, *Scriptural Truth About the Lord's Return,* pp. 72-73.
4. Floyd E. Hamilton, *The Basis of Millennial Faith,* pp. 23-24.

who began to proclaim the comforting hope and blessed promise of the coming of Christ; and since that time, the subject so long neglected has been studied and preached with increasing interest. Indeed, in the last two centuries, it seems to have risen (with the doctrine of salvation by simple faith in a crucified Savior) into somewhat the same prominence which it occupied in the early church.[5]

However, it should be pointed out that there isn't a single Reformer from Luther to Wesley who even remotely refers to a pretribulation rapture. Furthermore, such attempts to legitimize this teaching by linking it to the foundational truth of "salvation by faith" falls miserably short from scripturally justifying it.

Many pretribulationists seek to circumvent the problem with the relatively recent origin of pretribulationism by appealing to the "progressive revelation principle" in biblical interpretation. Advocates of this position claim that the primary reason for the marked absence of pretribulationist teachings prior to the 1830's is due to the fact that eschatological doctrine has been in a constant process of refinement since apostolic times. They stress that these "deeper truths" have only come to light in recent years as a greater degree of prophetic truth has gradually unfolded. As Stanton stated,

> During these past nineteen centuries, there has been a progressive refinement of the details of Christian theology, but not until the last one hundred years has eschatology come to the front to receive the major attention and scrutiny of foremost Bible scholars.[6]

He also added:

> If God used Darby and his associates to restore to the church doctrines long obscure and neglected, his name should be remembered with gratitude and not profaned as the originator of a twentieth century heresy.[7]

Hal Lindsey followed the same line of reasoning when he wrote:

> Christians after the early second century spent little time really defining prophetic truth until the middle of the nineteenth century. Then there seems to have been a great revival of interest in the prophetic themes of the Bible.[8]

---

5. William E. Blackstone, *Jesus Is Coming,* p. 36.
6. Gerald B. Stanton, *Kept From the Hour,* p. 223.
7. Ibid., p. 226.
8. Hal Lindsey, *The Late Great Planet Earth,* p. 170.

Walvoord also skirted the issue of historic authenticity by appealing to the "progressive refinement" theory:

> One of the commonly repeated reasons for opposing pre-tribulationism is that it is a new and novel doctrine beginning no earlier than Darby. Reese, who is usually regarded as the outstanding champion of opponents of pretribulationism, states categorically that it is "a series of doctrines that had never been heard of before," that is, before the nineteenth century. Reese charges that the followers of Darby "sought to overthrow what, since the Apostolic Age, have been considered by all pre-millennialists as established results!" It must be conceded that the advanced and detailed theology of pre-tribulationism is not found in the Fathers, but neither is any other detailed and "established" exposition of pre-millennialism. The development of the most important doctrines took centuries.[9]

Pretribulationists recognize the tremendous threat to their position by appeals to historic authenticity. Having only one meager defense in the form of the progressive refinement theory, they vigorously attack any challenge against this argument. They usually fall back upon the well-worn contention that not only was eschatological doctrine unrefined in the early church, but many other major doctrines were unformulated as well. For example, Pentecost wrote:

> Such an argument is an argument from silence. If the same line of reasoning were followed one would not accept the doctrine of justification by faith, for it was not clearly taught until the Reformation.[10]

However, this typical pretribulational argument is based upon very shallow assertions. The fact that "Justification by Faith," as well as many other cardinal doctrines, was clearly embraced and comprehended by the body of Christendom is patently revealed in the New Testament. The doctrine of "Justification by Faith," for example, is comprehensively covered in both the epistle to the Romans and the Galatians. This pretribulationist defense could be likened to the proverbial ostrich who buries his head in the sand rather than face the facts of reality. They are simply begging the issue on this point. Though, admittedly, doctrine has undergone certain refinements through the centuries, you can't rationally refine something that

9. John P. Walvoord, *The Rapture Question,* p. 50.
10. J. Dwight Pentecost, *Things to Come,* p. 166.

never existed. According to the Bible, the only one who is really capable of creating something out of nothing is God.

We have reviewed a few selected quotes from both "post" and "pre" tribulationists who frankly acknowledge that pretribulationism is a recent innovation in prophetic interpretation. Though some supporters of pretribulationism maintain that the doctrine can be traced to the earliest periods of church history, many openly admit that it was unheard of among the church fathers, the Reformers, or prior to the 1830's.

Neither the scriptures nor the position of the early church, stated or implied, lends any basis of support for a pretribulational concept. There isn't the slightest shred of evidence that this teaching ever existed, even in seed form. Pretribulationism is not a refinement of New Testament teaching, but a gross aberration of eschatological truth, and a teaching which lacks a reliable, historic pedigree.

The Early Church Writings

However, since some maintain that pretribulationism is an ancient teaching deeply rooted in the earliest antiquities of church history, we must examine the prophetic traditions of the church to determine whether or not this is true. A basic survey of the historic development of eschatological doctrine can greatly assist us in providing a solid framework for properly addressing the issue of pretribulationism.

In spite of the earnest endeavors of pretribulationists to find some shreds of support for a pretrib rapture in the writings of the early church, their labors have been consistently unsuccessful. A careful study of post-apostolic literature points up a glaring absence of anything remotely resembling a pretribulation rapture concept. In his survey of church history, Ladd commented on this point as follows:

> We can find no trace of pretribulationism in the early church, and no modern pretribulationist has successfully proved that this particular doctrine was held by any of the church fathers or students of the Word before the nineteenth century.[11]

A review of Ante-Nicene writings overwhelmingly substantiates the reality of this statement. Neither the writings of Clement of Rome

---

11. George E. Ladd, *The Blessed Hope,* p. 31.

(30-100 A.D.), "The Epistle to Barnabas" (130 A.D.), "The Shepherd of Hermas" (150 A.D.), "The Didache" (150 A.D.), Ignatius (50-115 A.D.), Polycarp (70-167 A.D.), Papias (80-163 A.D.), Pothinus (87-177 A.D.), Justyn Martyr (100-168 A.D.), Melito of Sardis (100-170 A.D.), Hegisippus (130-190 A.D.), Tatian (130-190 A.D.), Irenaeus (140-202 A.D.), Tertullian (150-220 A.D.), Hippolytus (160-240 A.D.), Cyprian (200-258 A.D.), Commodian (200-270 A.D.), Nepos (230-280 A.D.), Coracion (230-280 A.D.), Victorinus (240-303 A.D.), Methodius (250-311 A.D.), or Lactantius (240-330 A.D.) lend support to the validity of a pretribulation rapture. Furthermore, there isn't the slightest trace of a pretrib concept in the literature of many others who could be cited from this period.

In referring to these writings, I am not endeavoring to establish the "church fathers" as the last word on prophetic truth. Our final court of appeal must always be the revelation of scripture. The Word of God must, ultimately, be the deciding touchstone of all truth. However, while we should never be bound to the strict confines of tradition, tradition can play an important role in helping us determine the reliability of a teaching. As Ladd noted,

> While tradition does not provide authority, it would nevertheless be difficult to suppose that God had left his people in ignorance of an essential truth for nineteen centuries.[12]

Church tradition does play a deserving part in the consideration of a teaching's authenticity, especially when that teaching appears to be of fairly recent origin. Gundry's comments at this point are worthy of consideration:

> The novelty of an eschatological view requires that evidence put forward in its favor be weightier than usual since it is unlikely that saintly and learned scholars or the mass of pious Christians should for centuries have misconstrued the teachings of scripture on so important a point as the blessed hope. On the other hand, the antiquity of a view weighs in its favor, especially when that antiquity reaches back to the apostolic age. For those who received their doctrine first-hand from the apostles and from those who heard them stood in a better position to judge what was apostolic doctrine than we who are many centuries removed.[13]

---

12. Ibid., p. 20.
13. Robert H. Gundry, *The Church and the Tribulation,* p. 172.

In light of the complete absence of historic support for a pretribulation rapture concept among the writings of the Ante-Nicene period, it is understandable why its many proponents so commonly circumvent the issue of antiquity. However, not all pretribulationists evade the issue. Some attempt to defend its historic authenticity on the supposed grounds that it did exist, in incipient form, in the prophetic consciousness of the time. Claims are often laid upon the belief that the writings of the early church fathers indirectly support the concept of a pretribulation rapture. They base this argument on imminency. For example, Dwight Pentecost stated that,

> This doctrine of imminence, or "at any moment coming," is not a new doctrine with Darby, as is sometimes charged, although he did clarify, systematize, and popularize it.[14]

Pretribulationists sometimes contend that since the early fathers believed in an imminent, "any moment" return of Christ, that their belief undergirds the concept of a rapture of the church prior to the appearance of the antichrist.

However, even a casual survey of patristic literature proves that though the early church did indeed encourage a spirit of expectancy for Christ's return, they did not support a secret, "any moment" coming of Christ to rescue the saints before the tribulation. They believed that certain distinguishable events would first have to transpire. Therefore, the arguments of pretribulationists concerning "imminency" falls flat. Not a single writer suggests an imminent coming of Christ before an intervening tribulation period. The subject of imminency will be comprehensively covered in Chapter Ten.

Prophetic Trends

The controversy surrounding the chronology of the rapture in relationship to the second coming can be brought into clearer focus by briefly examining the historic developments in prophetic interpretation. Prophetic perspectives have undergone a series of changes over the last 1900 years. They have been in a relative state of flux since apostolic times. During extended periods, specific viewpoints were overwhelmingly embraced, while at other seasons there tended to be an overlapping of eschatological perspectives.

---

14. J. Dwight Pentecost, *Things to Come*, p. 203.

Though not all writers during the Patristic period (100-400 A.D.) expressed millenarian (or chiliastic) views, the overwhelming consensus was premillennial with a universally embraced postribulational emphasis. As Gundry commented:

Every Ante-Nicene writer who touches in any detail upon the tribulation, resurrection, rapture, or second coming displays a posttribulational persuasion.[15]

Though they embraced a strong spirit of expectancy regarding the second coming, they anticipated Christ's advent only after a series of specific, prophetic events had been fulfilled. They did not believe in an "any moment" return of Christ, as many pretribulationists claim. Though their posttribulational expectation was futurist, it should be clarified that their futurism was based on the assumption that certain distinguishable events would soon transpire. They generally did not believe in a prolonged postponement of such outstanding events as the appearance of antichrist, the beginning of a tribulation period, and the second coming of Christ—certainly not in terms of two millennia.

The concept of a pretribulation rapture was totally foreign to their eschatological understanding. Not the slightest hint of a pretribulation rapture can be detected in the literature of this time frame. The historic hope of the church during the first three centuries was clearly anchored upon the return of Christ after the church had suffered persecution and tribulation at the hands of antichrist.

Medieval Eschatology

Towards the end of the post-apostolic period, the expectation of antichrist's soon appearance prior to Christ's return gradually diminished. Scholars began to spiritualize the millennium into the present age. Many confined it to an indefinite period before the end of this age. Some believed that the end would coincide with the year 1000 A.D. They rejected the typical millenarianism which places the millennial reign after the rapture of the church. They basically taught that the thousand years began with Christ's public ministry, and continues in effect until the second coming. Augustine took the lead

---

15. Robert H. Gundry, *The Church and the Tribulation*, p. 178.

23

in establishing an eschatological framework for supporting the various forms of amillennialism in his famous work entitled, *The City of God.*

Pentecost capsulized Augustine's conclusions as follows:

> Thus Augustine made several important assertions which molded eschatological thinking: (1) He denied that the millennium would follow the second advent, (2) he held that the millennium would fall in the inter-advent period, and (3) he taught that the church is the kingdom and there would be no literal fulfillment of the promises made to Israel. These interpretations formed the central core of the eschatological system that dominated theological thinking for centuries.[16]

The premillennial schemes of such outstanding Ante-Nicene writers as Irenaeus, Tertullian, and Justyn Martyr gave way to Augustine's amillennial emphasis. His prophetic ideas formed a strong basis of support for the growing trend towards amillennialism, and became the prevailing viewpoint within the Roman church. Though premillennialism lingered in isolated sectors, the amillennial method dominated the prophetic scene for several centuries and was eventually adopted by the majority of Protestant Reformers during the Reformation period.

Reformation Eschatology

During the Dark Ages of Roman Catholic supremacy, and continuing throughout the Reformation period, the overwhelming view espoused by the Reformers was based upon the Historic perspective. Christians tended to view the Book of Revelation against the backdrop of the historical evolution of the church. The Reformers enthusiastically embraced the Historist school, and found in the antichrist a clear parallel with the papal system and the Roman church.

Though the followers of this school believed in a posttribulational coming of Christ, they did not believe in a personal antichrist who would appear for a brief period of time at the end of this age and wreak havoc upon the church for three and a half years. To them, the antichrist was a counterfeit system of apostasy which they scripturally identified as the Roman papacy. Neither did they believe in an

---

16. J. Dwight Pentecost, *Things to Come,* p. 382.

isolated period of "Great Tribulation" during the closing seven years of this dispensation. Instead, they viewed tribulation as one of the distinguishing features of the entire church age.

They interpreted the 1260 days, or 3-1/2 years, mentioned in Revelation as twelve hundred and sixty years of church history before the end could arrive. This "day-year theory" was a hallmark of their interpretive system. To them, the Book of Revelation was a symbolic picture book representing the unfolding drama of the church age. They saw in the seals, vials, and trumpets the symbolized drama of unfolding church history.

The Reformers so heartily advocated the Historic school of prophetic interpretation that it has commonly been referred to as "The Protestant Interpretation." Many contemporary students of biblical prophecy are unaware of the immense significance and sway which this particular school of interpretation exerted upon the development of eschatological perspectives. It dominated the field of prophetic inquiry for centuries. In fact, it played a strategic part in the battle cry of the Reformers, and many supporters of the Historic school of interpretation laid down their lives in defense of this prophetic perspective.

Some of the prominent individuals who held this view from the twelfth through the eighteenth century were: Eberhard II, John Foxe, John Wyclif, Walter Brute, Sir John Oldcastle, John Huss, Martin Luther, Andreas Osiander, Nicolaus Von Amsdorf, Philipp Melanchthon, John Calvin, John Knox, John Napier, Huldreich Zwingli, Heinrich Bullinger, Theodor Bibliander, Alfonsus Conradus, William Tyndale, Nicholas Ridley, John Bradford, John Hooper, Hugh Latimer, Thomas Cranmer, William Fluke, Sir Isaac Newton, Johann Bengel, John Wesley, and Andreas Helwig.

While most of the Reformers embraced amillennialist views, a few espoused premillennial sentiments. However, even those of the premillennial persuasion clung tenaciously to the historic interpretation. It should be pointed out that the premillennial views of this time frame were vastly different from the contemporary forms of premillennialism popularized since the 1830's. Present day premillennialism is generally a radical departure from the historic premillennialism of the Reformation and post-Reformation era. The principle difference lies in the inordinate emphasis on a heavily futuristic outline of prophetic events. There are numerous elements in modern forms of premillennialism which were unheard of prior to the nineteenth century. One of the most significant differences involves the concept of a pretribulation rapture.

Though the prophetic viewpoints varied from amillennialism to premillennialism, every one retained the Historic school of eschatological interpretation. It was an integral facet of their prophetic systems. The heavy emphasis on futurism had not yet crept into the prophetic mainstream. Futhermore, none of these men believed in, or even remotely entertained, the notion of a pretribulation rapture. It was an alien concept in their eschatological tradition.

2

The Rise and Spread
of Pretribulationism

Whitbyism

At the beginning of the eighteenth century, a prophetic trend
emerged which would have an indirect impact upon the eventual
development of pretribulationism. In 1706, a new interpretation was
formulated by Daniel Whitby (1638-1726), an Englishman who taught
that the world would eventually be evangelized, that the church would
rule the world, and that Christ would return after a glorious millennial
period. He basically believed in the progressive betterment of the
world through the positive influences of the church. He postulated
the teaching that the church would usher in a millennial reign upon
the earth prior to Christ's second advent. His teachings helped popularize the postmillennial school of prophecy. During the eighteenth
century, postmillennialism was enthusiastically embraced by many,
especially in Europe.

Others who embraced postmillennialism, or variations thereof, were
John Wesley, Johann Bengel, and Jonathan Edwards. However, in

spite of their postmillennial persuasions, these men continued to retain the historic perspective, and the idea of a secret rapture was completely foreign to their prophetic systems.

Whitby's postmillennialism captured the hearts of the Christian community during the 1700's, and indirectly contributed to minimizing the importance and sense of expectancy for the Lord's return. As a consequence of his teaching, the glorious doctrine of the second coming was relegated to a position of neglect and obscurity.

The Prophetic Awakening

The early nineteenth century marked an important juncture in the development of prophetic interpretation. At the turn of the century (1800), a strong reaction arose which reasserted the importance of the personal return of Christ. Whitbyism, which had dominated the prophetic landscape for over a century, resulted in a prophetic backlash which would dramatically alter the course of prophetic interpretation. Once again, the doctrine of the second coming was thrust into the forefront of prophetic importance. It seemed as if a fresh breath of air had blown upon the subject of prophetic inquiry. This prophetic counter-reaction gave birth to the "prophetic awakening."

Two outstanding features characterize this period: 1) A strong reaction against Whitby's postmillennialism arose, and 2) A gradual rejection of the historic method in favor of futuristic premillennialism. Both of these distinguishing features would eventually dovetail, the result being the birth of pretribulationism. The formation of a pretribulation rapture theory is deeply embedded in the developments of this period.

This period witnessed an increasing defection from the ranks of the Historic school and a renewed interest in futurism. The Futurist school taught that the antichrist would be a satanically-inspired world ruler at the end of this age who would inflict intense persecution upon the church during the Great Tribulation, and at the end of that Tribulation, Christ would return to deliver the church, punish antichrist, translate the righteous dead, and establish His millennial kingdom upon earth. Though this brand of futuristic premillennialism was increasingly in vogue, the concept of a pretribulation rapture was still unheard of prior to 1830.

Though the "day-year theory" was still popular, it began to lose credibility after predicted events based upon historist's calculations failed to materialize. The "day-year theory" gradually fell into disrepute due to the often outlandish and unsuccessful attempts at datesetting. The extremes of the Historic school helped legitimize the accelerated shift to futurism.

Historic Futurism?

As a sideline, many contemporary futurists claim that this shift was simply a return to the historic beliefs of the early church. For example, Ladd comments:

> The futuristic interpretation was essentially a return to the method of prophetic truth found in the early fathers, essential to which is the teaching that the antichrist will be a satanically-inspired world ruler at the end of the age who would inflict severe persecution upon the church during the Great Tribulation.[1]

This perspective is often appealed to by modern premillennialists in discounting the historic beliefs embraced by premillennialists, amillennialists, and postmillennialists prior to the 1830's. However, this point requires a measurable qualification. While the early church was generally premillennial, posttribulational, and futuristic in their eschatological beliefs, present day futurism is not synonymous with the earlier forms of futurism. There is a distinguishable difference in their futurist outlook. When comparing the futurism of the early nineteenth century with the futurism of the early church, Froom noted:

> This is full-fledged futurism, but such was not the belief of the early church. And the early Christians cannot justly be claimed futurists. They did not anticipate the expiration of a long church era before the beginning of these fulfillments. They saw most of the prophecies as future because, as has been remarked "in their days so little history had yet come to pass in fulfillment of the Apocalypse." They were simply adherents of a continuous-historical approach.[2]

The early church was strongly futuristic in their prophetic outlook because they were poised on the threshold of the entire church age before the commencement of the significant prophetic events which loomed before them. As Woodrow pointed out,

---

1. George E. Ladd, *The Blessed Hope,* p. 37.
2. LeRoy E. Froom, *The Prophetic Faith of Our Fathers, Vol. IV,* p. 425; cited from *The Millennium in the Church,* D. H. Dromminga, pp. 333-335, 252, 253.

Some say that the people in the early church were futurists. Of course. In the opening days of the New Testament church, all of these things were future. But that does not mean these things are still future almost 2,000 years later! Futurists today cannot truly link their teachings with those of the early church, for most present day futurists hold the view— not only that most of the prophecies were in the future at the beginning of the Christian era—but that they will still be in the future at the end of the Christian era. This is quite different.[3]

This is an important point for contemporary pretribulationists, premillennialists, and posttribulationists to consider, especially those who cling to this argument in defense of current, futuristic chronologies.

The Roman Catholic Contribution

A significant contributing factor in the development of both futurism and pretribulationism can be traced to a very unlikely source, as far as most fundamental Christians are concerned. Surprisingly, the eventual mass defection from the ranks of the Historic school actually originated in the bosom of the Roman Catholic church. Much of the growing emphasis upon futurism during the early nineteenth century had been quietly borrowed from Jesuit theologians. Ribera, along with others, had quietly cultivated the fertile soil from which futurism would eventually burst into full bloom. As Guiness commented,

> In its present form (the futurist interpretation) it may be said to have originated at the end of the sixteenth century with the Jesuit Ribera, who moved . . . to relieve the Papacy from the terrible stigma cast upon it by the Protestant interpretation, and tried to do so by referring their prophecies to the distant future . . .[4]

The cradle for contemporary futurism was actually constructed by Catholic theologians opposed to the Reformers' historical method of interpretation.

Throughout the Reformation and post-Reformation periods, Protestants had rallied around the historic method of interpretation in exposing the corruption of the papal system. In fact, this belief was one of the outstanding tenets of the Protestant Reformation. The twofold truth that "the just shall live by faith" and the claim

---

3. Ralph Woodrow, *Great Prophecies of the Bible*, p. 197.
4. H. Grattan Guiness, *The Approaching End of the Age*, p. 100.

that the Papacy characterized the antichrist system represented the battle cry of the Reformation. As Froom stressed,

> The entire Reformation rested on this twofold testimony. The Reformers were unanimous in its acceptance. And it was this interpretation of prophecy that lent emphasis to their reformation action. It led them to protest against Rome with extraordinary strength and undaunted courage. It nerved them to resist to the utmost the claims of the apostate church. It sustained them at the martyr's stake. Verily, this was the rallying point and the battle cry that made the Reformation unconquerable.[5]

However, Rome was not without its champions. She quickly retaliated by postulating the futuristic method of prophetic interpretation in order to undermine the Protestant position. As the Encyclopedia Britannica stated: "Under the stress of the Protestant attack there arose new methods on the Papal side."[6] The primary purpose of this counter-interpretation was to divert attention away from the Papacy and discredit the Protestant interpretation. With the introduction of her brand of futurism, Rome was able to gradually parry the sword of the Reformers.

Jesuit theologians were the first to rush to the aid of Rome. As Allis commented, "The futurist interpretation is traced back to the Jesuit Ribera (A.D. 1580) whose aim was to disprove the claim of the Reformers that the Pope was the Antichrist."[7] Francisco Ribera (1537-1591) of Salamanca, Spain, published a 500-page commentary on the Revelation in 1590 as a rebuttal to the Reformers. He restricted the bulk of Revelation to the end times, rather than applying it to the history of the church. He claimed that antichrist would be an individual who would rebuild Jersulam, abolish the Christian religion, deny Christ, persecute the church, and dominate the world for three and a half years.

Robert Bellarmine (1542-1621), an Italian Cardinal and Jesuit controversialist, further promoted Ribera's teachings. "Although Ribera launched the Futurist system of interpretation, it was popularized and made to register by the astute Cardinal Bellarmine, with his effective phrasings and polemical power . . ."[8] He vigorously defended

---

5. LeRoy E. Froom, *The Prophetic Faith of Our Fathers, Vol. 2*, pp. 243-244.
6. *Encyclopedia Britannica, Eleventh Edition, Vol. 23*, p. 243.
7. Oswald T. Allis, *Prophecy and the Church*, p. 297.
8. LeRoy E. Froom, *The Prophetic Faith of Our Fathers, Vol. 2*, p. 495.

this futuristic perspective, and was the most outstanding adversary of the Protestant position. This perspective soon gained wide acceptance among Roman Catholics. However, the Protestant interpretation continued to hold ground until the nineteenth century when cracks began to appear in their prophetic bulwarks.

Both of these men, unbeknownst to Protestants at the time, were sowing the seeds of futurism which would spring up two and a half centuries later. As Froom commented,

> Thus in Ribera's commentary was laid the foundation for that great structure of Futurism, built upon and enlarged by those who followed, until it became the common Catholic position. And then, wonder of wonders, in the nineteenth century this Jesuit scheme of interpretation came to be adopted by a growing number of Protestants, until today Futurism, amplified and adorned with the rapture theory, has become the generally accepted belief of the fundamentalist's wing of popular Protestantism.[9]

In the early nineteenth century, another Spanish Jesuit further cultivated the fields of futurism. He would have a more immediate impact upon the unfolding events of the prophetic awakening than either Ribera or Bellarmine. His name was Emanuel de Lacunza (1731-1801). He would play an instrumental role in helping influence such key figures in the "prophetic awakening" as Dr. Samuel Maitland and Edward Irving.

His work entitled, *The Coming of the Messiah in Glory and Majesty,* was first published in 1812, eleven years after his death. He had written his work under the fictitious penname of Rabbi Ben Ezra. He employed this alias to conceal his true identity in order to make his writings more palatable to Protestant readers. His work represented another countermeasure by the church of Rome to relieve the pressures imposed upon it by the Protestant interpretation. Through subtle subterfuge, Lacunza managed to take the heat off Rome by refocusing the Protestants' attention away from the Romish system and on to a highly futuristic perspective. He restricted the prophetic fulfillments of the Revelation to the very end of the age. He taught that the appearance of the antichrist and the fulfillment of all prophecies concerning them are still in the future, and that they will all be fulfilled in a brief period of time prior to Christ's return in glory.

---

9. LeRoy E. Froom, *The Prophetic Faith of Our Fathers, Vol. 2,* p. 493.

In 1816, a complete Spanish edition of Lacunza's work was published in London and soon after found its way into the receptive hands of strategic individuals who would play a prominent role in the development of futurism and pretribulationist teaching. His writings, along with those of Ribera's, exerted a tremendous influence upon the emerging futurists of the early nineteenth century. Their works acted as catalysts in stimulating the spread of futurism.

One of the earliest Protestants to draw from Ribera and Lacunza was Samuel R. Maitland. As Ladd noted:

> This futurist interpretation with its personal antichrist and three and a half year tribulation did not take root in the Protestant church until the early nineteenth century. The first Protestant to adopt it was S. R. Maitland.[10]

Dr. Maitland was the curator to the Archbishop of Canterbury. In 1826 he shocked the Protestant community of England with a pamphlet entitled, *An Enquiry Into the Ground on Which the Prophetic Period of Daniel and St. John Has Been Supposed to Consist of 1260 Years.* In it he attacked the still popular "day-year theory" held by the historical interpreters. He contended that the number 1260 did not represent years, but 1260 literal days of tribulation prior to Christ's return. He consigned the book of Revelation to a strict, futuristic setting just prior to Christ's return. He eventually wrote over fifty books attacking the historic method.

Maitland's pioneer efforts were soon followed by others. Among them were James Todd and William Burgh. Todd was a professor of Hebrew at Dublin, and a devoted follower of Maitland's views. He published over 500 pages of lectures defending futuristic beliefs. William Burgh also contributed to this "wave of futurism" by publishing the first systematic treatment of the futurist interpretation in 1835.

However, none of these early forerunners of futurism were pretribulationists.

> Those early futurists followed a pattern of prophetic events similar to that found in the early fathers, with the necessary exception that Rome was not the first kingdom. In fact, they appeal to the fathers against

---

10. George E. Ladd, *The Blessed Hope,* p. 38.

the popular historical interpretation for support of their basic view. A pretribulation rapture is utterly unknown by these men . . . .[11]

As of yet, pretribulationism had not yet surfaced.

Prophetic Popularity

This period experienced a revolutionary resurgence in prophetic interest. There was a deluge of prophetic literature. Numerous books, periodicals, and tracts were penned in support of prophetic exposition and the heralding of Christ's soon return. Even the daily newspapers devoted columns to prophetic subjects. One of the prominent periodicals was called the *Investigator* (1831-1836), edited by J. W. Brooks. The last volume in the series contained an exhaustive "Dictionary of Writers on the Prophecies" which included over 2,100 titles of books on prophetic subjects. This figure attests to the voluminous amount of prophetic material published during this period.

Coupled with the surge in prophetic literature was the popularity of prophetic conferences. One of the earliest was sponsored by a wealthy banker by the name of Henry Drummond. From 1826 to 1830 a series of prophetic conferences were held at his palatial villa at Albury Park, southwest of London. The renewed interest in prophetic inquiry also gave birth to similar meetings at Lady Theodsia Powerscourt's mansion south of Dublin.

Two key individuals participated in these conferences and soon became leaders in this prophetic revival. They were Edward Irving and John Darby. Irving was a regular speaker at the Albury Park meeting where he had a powerful influence upon the trend towards futurism. Darby, on the other hand, was the main spokesman at the Powerscourt conferences, where his leadership and influence gradually exerted itself. Both of these figures exerted a tremendous influence upon the direction of prophetic development.

It was at the Powerscourt meetings that the distinctive elements of a pretribulation rapture were introduced into the mainstream of prophetic awareness. As Froom remarked:

> It was in the conferences held at Powerscourt castle in Ireland (1830 and onward) that a new theory was formulated which laid the foundation for a whole new system of belief. This was based on the "rapture"

---

11. Ibid., p. 39.

of the church—as referring to the resurrected and living saints being "caught up" to meet the Lord (I Thessalonians 4:17)—placed before the final tribulation, leaving the rest of the world's populace to go through a literal 3-1/2 years of persecution by a future personal Antichrist, before the destruction of that tyrant by the glorious Appearance of Christ.[12]

As the momentum of the "prophetic awakening" mounted, multitudes crossed over to futuristic beliefs. In the midst of this prophetic migration, Irving and Darby stepped to the forefront and for the first time injected the novel teaching of a pretribulation rapture. Irving and Darby soon became aggressive proponents of the pretribulation theory. Each played an integral part in the early development of futurist and pretribulationist beliefs.

Edward Irving

Edward Irving was born in Scotland in 1792. He was a brilliant young man who managed to attend Edinburgh University at the age of thirteen. After graduating with an M.A. in 1809, he was licensed as a Presbyterian minister at the age of twenty. In 1822, he became the pastor of the Caledonia Chapel. He soon became one of the most eloquent preachers of his day.

He was born when postmillennialism was still popular. With the prophetic awakening of the early 1800's, postmillennialism was largely discarded in favor of premillennial beliefs with a strong historic base. Irving was influenced by this type of premillennialism until he discovered the emerging writings of Lacunza, which had exerted such a strong sway upon early futurists such as Maitland. Lacunza's futurism had a profound impact upon the evolution of Irving's prophetic beliefs.

Lacunza's Spanish edition of *The Coming of the Messiah in Glory and Majesty* had attracted so much attention in London circles that an English version was soon in demand. The labor of translating this version was assumed by Irving. Lacunza's challenge to the historical method of interpretation helped catapult Irving into the futurist camp.

Soon after, he began to promulgate his futuristic beliefs at the Albury conferences. However, the concept of a pretribulation rapture

---

12. LeRoy E. Froom, *The Prophetic Faith of Our Fathers, Vol. 4*, p. 422.

did not seem to surface in Irving's teachings until the early 1830's, even though the futuristic groundwork had been carefully prepared at the Albury conferences. However, it has been clearly authenticated that Irving was one of the first to suggest this theory. He is frequently accredited with being a major accomplice in the birth of pretribulational teaching. For example, Gundry writes:

> Pretribulationism arose in the mid-nineteenth century. The likelihood is that Edward Irving was the first to suggest the pretribulation rapture, or at least the seminal thought behind it.[13]

One of the earliest records tracing the origins of the pretrib rapture to Irving was referred to by Harold Rowden:

> As early as September, 1830, a distinction was drawn in an article in *The Morning Watch* (an Irvingite journal) between the epiphany and the "advent" or "parousia" of Christ. The former was interpreted as His appearance in the sky which would strike terror into the hearts of unbelievers and would be the signal for the resurrection of dead saints and the changing of them and the living saints in the act of rapture of I Thessalonians 4:16, 17. The advent, comprising the return of Christ and the saints to the earth bringing judgment to the nations, was expected to follow. The view that the saints would be caught up to heaven, like Enoch and Elijah, was obviously a development of the idea that they would be sheltered in some "little sanctuary" from the outpouring of Divine judgment upon the earth.[14]

Though dispensationalists, like Walvoord, go to great lengths to discredit any association of a pretrib origin with Edward Irving,[15] their attempts are neither fruitful nor convincing. Pretribulational links to Irving can be substantiated from a variety of sources; however, the most incriminating is from Irving himself. The fact that Irving embraced pretribulational sentiments is confirmed by an article he penned in *The Morning Watch*[16] in which he claimed that under the sixth trumpet, in the midst of revolution and bloodshed, the church baptized with the Holy Ghost (that is, the Irvingite or Catholic

---

13. Robert H. Gundry, *The Church and the Tribulation*, p. 185.

14. Harold H. Rowden, *The Origins of the Brethren*, p. 16.

15. John F. Walvoord, *The Blessed Hope and the Tribulation*, pp. 42-45.

16. Edward Irving, "An Interpretation of the Fourteenth Chapter of the Apocalypse," *The Morning Watch*, Vol. 5, pp. 308, 309, 323, Cf. the next installment in *Vol 6*, pp. 18, 27.

Apostolic Church) will, like the two witnesses, after three and one-half years of keeping down the future antichrist, be slain and ascend into glory, leading with them the righteous dead and those who have not been called upon to seal their testimony with their blood. Afterwards, the antichrist will emerge (the "let," or church, being removed). Finally, this church of the first-born (the man-child of Revelation 12), being with Christ in the cloud of His glory, will come with Him to pour out the seven vials upon God's enemies.

Another frequently quoted reference associating the pretribulation rapture with Irving is the famous quote of Dr. Samuel P. Tregelles. He was an early Brethren scholar, and contemporary with the earliest beginnings of pretribulationism. He also rejected this novel teaching as being scripturally unwarranted. He claimed that the belief in a secret pretribulation rapture originated around the year 1832. He also stated that,

> I am not aware that there was any definite teaching that there would be a secret rapture of the church at a secret coming, until this was given as an "utterance" in Mr. Irving's church, from what was there received as being the voice of the Spirit. But whether any one ever asserted such a thing or not, it was from that supposed revelation that the modern doctrine and modern phraseology respecting it arose. It came not from Holy Scripture, but from that which falsely pretended to be the Spirit of God . . . .[17]

In Murray's treatment of the development of the pretribulation rapture, he indirectly links its origins to Edward Irving:

> At Albury and in Irving's London congregation a curious belief, practically unknown in earlier church history, had arisen, namely that Christ's appearing before the millennium is to be in two stages, the first, a secret "rapture" removing the church before the "Great Tribulation" smites the earth, the second his coming with his saints to set up his kingdom. This idea comes into full prominence in Darby.[18]

In 1828, Irving concluded that the spiritual gifts of the apostolic period were intended for the church of all ages. He penned numerous books and pamphlets defending this contention, along with heralding the imminent return of Christ. His predominant emphasis upon

---

17. Samuel P. Tregelles, *The Hope of Christ's Second Coming,* p. 35.
18. Iain H. Murray, *The Puritan Hope,* p. 200.

prophecy was reflected in such books as, *The Last Days: Their Character Evil* (1828), *Book of Revelation Interpreted* (1829), and *Daniel's Vision of the Four Beasts* (1829).

Shortly after advocating the restoration of spiritual gifts, he was placed on trial by the Presbyterian Church in 1832 for permitting unauthorized utterances of tongues and prophecy in his London church. He was censored and officially removed from the pastorate, whereupon he withdrew and formed the Catholic Apostolic Church. This was only his first confrontation with the established church.

In 1830, Irving wrote a tract suggesting that Christ had actually possessed a fallen human nature. A trial was eventually held on March 13, 1833, for Christological heresy, and Irving was deposed from the ministry. A short time later, he died of a broken heart on December 7, 1834, at the age of 42. Though his participation in the early development of pretribulationism was short-lived, his influence had a lasting impact upon the establishment of this doctrine. But it was John Darby who would be most responsible for proclaiming this teaching.

John Darby

Though Irving is repeatedly associated with the earliest origins of pretribulationism, Darby is accredited with being the driving force behind its spread. While all the salient features of Darby's teachings are found in Irving's initial suggestions, Darby became the principal spokesman for pretribulationist views.

> Though Irving apparently taught some kind of a secret rapture . . . it was JOHN NELSON DARBY that introduced it into the main current of prophetic interpretation. With slight differences on details, with possible additions here and there, the basic system formulated by Darby continues today in the secret rapture theory of dispensationalism.[19]

He was so intimately identified with this emerging belief that it has commonly been referred to as "Darbyism"—otherwise known as Dispensationalism. In fact, he has been called "the father of modern Dispensationalism."

Darby was born in London in 1800 at the very beginning of the prophetic awakening. He was highly educated and a prolific writer.

---

19. Ralph Woodrow, *Great Prophecies of the Bible,* p. 49.

During his life span, he penned over thirty volumes of 600 pages each on biblical topics.

Like Irving, Darby came into the world during a time of great prophetic flux. He was born at a season when Whitby's popular postmillennialism was beginning to be challenged. He originally embraced the historic premillennial school, but eventually shifted to the trend towards futurism during the mid 1820's.

Darby had started his career as a lawyer. However, he gave up his law practice in 1825 to become a deacon in the Anglican church. In 1826, he was ordained a priest. He soon became dissatisfied with the lethargic liberalism of the established church and, in 1827, he broke away to join the Brethren movement. Shortly thereafter, he became its dominant leader and helped shape its history.

The Brethren were a group of spiritual men who were fed up with the lukewarm condition of the church. Their movement originated in Dublin in 1825 and soon spread to England. The more prominent group was centered in Plymouth, England. Because of this, this group is often referred to as the "Plymouth Brethren." The Brethren devoted themselves primarily to prayer, fellowship, and the study of scripture. But a growing interest in prophetic inquiry soon arose within their ranks, and the movement soon became a vehicle for helping propagate Darby's teachings.

It was in the cradle of the Brethren movement that Darby's brand of futurism, embellished with a pretribulation rapture and other so-called "rediscovered truths," were refined and structured into dispensational theology.

However, it should be clarified that not all of the Brethren accepted Darby's teachings. His innovations generated repeated strife and disagreements within the ranks of Brethrenism. Some embraced Darby's modifications, while others clung tenaciously to the traditional historic premillennialism. Tregelles, one of the outstanding Greek scholars of his day, rejected Darby's pretrib rapture theory along with B. W. Newton, who labeled Darby's novelties as "the height of speculative nonsense." Other Brethren who rejected Darby's teachings outright or later renounced them were George Muller, Henry Craik, James Wright, Robert Chapman, and Henry W. Soltau. In fact, George Muller, the great man of prayer, stated that, "The time came when I had either to part from my Bible or part from John Darby.

I chose to keep my precious Bible and part from John Darby." Other outstanding contemporaries who rejected Darby's teachings as unscriptural were Charles H. Spurgeon and William Booth.

It should be pointed out that Darby's dispensational brand of futuristic premillennialism was a radical departure from the historic premillennialism taught prior to the 1830's, and a blatant reversal of established prophetic perspectives. As Reese noted:

> About 1830 . . . a new school arose within the fold of Premillennialism that sought to overthrow what, since the Apostolic Age, have been considered by all Pre-millennialists as established results, and to institute in their place a series of doctrines that had never been heard of before. The school I refer to is that of "The Brethren" or "Plymouth Brethren," founded by J. N. Darby.[20]

Furthermore, many of Darby's contemporary premillennialists strongly rejected his innovations. As Allis commented:

> . . . When these particular doctrines were announced . . . they were declared to be rediscovered truths which had been lost sight of since apostolic times; and they were vigorously opposed by many Premillennialists who regarded them as dangerous innovations. Consequently, it is important to remember that Premillennialism and Dispensationalism are not synonymous terms. All Dispensationalists are Premillenarians, but it is by no means true that all Premillenarians are Dispensationalists. Dispensationalists are futurists; they are also Pretribulationists. Many or most Premillenarians are to be classed as Historicists and Post-tribulationists.[21]

. Darby, along with his band of Brethren followers, claimed that they were simply teaching those "rediscovered truths" which had been taught by the apostles, but lost during the bulk of the church age. They often harbored an air of spiritual elitism, and held in subtle contempt those who failed to side with their beliefs.

> The Brethren boasted, from their very beginning in the nineteenth century, that their teachings represented a wide departure from the doctrines of their predecessors and contemporaries. According to them, all the prominent commentaries, all the church fathers, and even the Reformers, were deluded by "man-made doctrines," while only the

---

20. Alexander Reese, *The Approaching Advent of Christ,* p. 19.
21. Oswald T. Allis, *Prophecy and the Church,* p. 9.

Brethren were subject to and submissive to the Bible as the Word of God.[22]

Cox further added:

These alleged truths supposedly had been taught by the apostles, then lost sight of. Even the Great Reformers had not known of these doctrines. These "rediscovered truths" were, in fact, the direct opposite of all historic Christian teachings proclaimed by the Reformers and extant commentaries. Notice was given to the world at large that everyone should look at all previous post-apostolic teachings as false, and that only the "rediscovered truths" of the Brethren should be embraced.[23]

At the Powerscourt conferences, the Brethren, headed by Darby, began to formulize their prophetic concepts. As Ironside confirmed,

The precious truth of the Rapture of the church was brought to light, that is, the coming of the Lord in the air to take away His church before the great tribulation should begin on earth. These views brought out at Powerscourt castle not only largely formed the views of Brethren elsewhere, but as years went on obtained wide publication in (other) denominational circles, chiefly through the writings of such men as Darby. . . .[24]

It was at these meetings that pretribulationism achieved its first foothold. In these meetings, Darby gradually modified the futuristic perspective to include the teaching of a pretrib rapture. The rising tide of Darby's futurism soon gained momentum and became a steady flood which eventually engulfed the prophetic consciousness of both England and much of North America.

Those who have traced the earliest origins of the pretrib rapture claim that Darby first introduced this teaching at the Powerscourt meetings in 1833.[25] However, it is highly unlikely that Darby had anything to do with the actual creation of this doctrine. It seems that he borrowed it from his repeated contacts with the Irvingites. But one thing is certain. Darby did become the torchbearer for this teaching, and gave the greatest impetus to the systematic pretribulationism and dispensationalism which is embraced by millions today.

---

22. William E. Cox, *An Examination of Dispensationalism,* p. 1.
23. Ibid., p. 8.
24. H. A. Ironside, *A Historical Sketch of the Brethren Movement,* p. 23.
25. Ernest R. Sandeen, *The Roots of Fundamentalism,* p. 38.

The Macdonald Clan

In retracing the trail of pretribulational beliefs, one thing stands out as certain: it had its beginning no earlier than the early 1830's. For well over a century, historians have endeavored to pinpoint the precise origins of pretribulationism. It has generally been attributed to Edward Irving and John Darby. These individuals stand out as the ones most commonly associated with the earliest origins of this belief. As an example, F. Roy Coad affirmed that,

> Into the futurist system both Darby and Irving had injected a further refinement, based upon a detailed attempt to reconcile the different parts of the New Testament which they considered to be relevant. In their view, the second Advent would take place in two stages: First, there would be a quiet appearance—the "presence" of Christ, when all true Christians, the true church, would be removed from the earth. This was the "rapture of the saints."[26]

Some have variously attributed its inception to either the Plymouth Brethren,[27] Lacunza,[28] or to a strange "utterance" in Irving's London church.[29] Still others have maintained that this teaching simply existed as "free elements in the religious atmosphere" of the time, and suggest the possibility that it was being simultaneously circulated by a variety of individuals, both identifiable and anonymous.[30]

Though numerous writers have touched, in general terms, upon the question of exact origins, few have endeavored to present any comprehensive information concerning this crucial subject. A handful of scholars have attempted to be more precise in pinpointing the actual source of this teaching. For example, in LeRoy E. Froom's exhaustive work entitled, *The Prophetic Faith of Our Fathers,* he wrote,

> . . . the "utterances" appeared, first in Scotland and then in London, in 1831, and were received as the gift of prophecy. During Irving's first tour of Scotland, some young woman had been healed by prayer. Later when supernatural manifestations began to appear, they claimed to have the gift of tongues. A favorable report from a delegation of

---

26. F. Roy Coad, *A History of the Brethren Movement,* p. 63.
27. William E. Cox, *An Examination of Dispensationalism,* p. 1.
28. John L. Bray, *The Origin of the Pre-Tribulation Rapture Teaching,* pp. 1-12.
29. Samuel P. Tregelles, *The Hope of Christ's Second Coming,* p. 35.
30. Ernest R. Sandeen, *The Roots of Fundamentalism,* p. 90.

Irving's congregation led to the organization of meetings to seek the restoration of the gifts.[31]

Several important statements are referred to in Froom's quote which demand the researcher's attention. They include "Scotland," "a young women," and "Irving."

John A. Anderson, an English author, was even more specific in establishing the actual origin of pretribulationism. In his work entitled, *Heralds of the Dawn,* he asserted that a Miss M.M. had originated the two-stage coming theory in March of 1830 in Great Britain.[32]

One of the most comprehensive attempts to identify the actual origins of a pretribulational rapture teaching can be linked to the laborious research of Dave MacPherson. We are indebted to him for his exhaustive efforts in tracing the actual origins of this teaching. His book entitled, *The Incredible Cover-Up,* is a recommended must for all those who are seriously endeavoring to get to the bottom of the pretribulation issue. According to MacPherson's findings, the first utterance of a pretrib concept did not originate in Irving's London church, as some have contended, but in a private housemeeting in the spring of 1830, during a charismatic revival which had broken out in Scotland.

This Scottish revival generated a great deal of interest and controversy and attracted many curiosity seekers, among whom were John Darby and a delegation dispatched from Irving's church. This delegation had been commissioned at the last Albury conference in July of 1830 to investigate this phenomenon. Both Irving and Darby, as we have seen, would soon become fervent advocates of this new teaching. It is interesting to note that in September of 1830, shortly after Irving's delegation had returned from investigating the Scottish revival, an Irvingite paper called *The Morning Watch* drew one of the earliest public distinctions between the two phases of Christ's return in an article entitled, *On the Epiphany of Our Lord Jesus Christ and the Gathering of His Elect.*[33]

The key figures behind this Scottish revival were the Macdonald family of Port Glasgow, Scotland. It was one of the sisters in this

---

31. LeRoy E. Froom, *The Prophetic Faith of Our Fathers, Vol. III,* p. 525.
32. John A. Anderson, *Heralds of the Dawn,* p. 40.
33. Harold H. Rowdon, *The Origins of the Brethren,* pp. 30, 31.

family (Margaret Macdonald) who was responsible for the first revelation concerning a pretrib rapture.

Dr. Robert Norton, an English clergyman, affirmed that it was a member of the Macdonald family who had originated the two-stage theory in March of 1830. Norton's information was not acquired through second-hand rumor or hearsay. He was both an eye and ear witness to Margaret's novel teaching.

When news reached London of the Scottish revival, Norton, along with others such as John Darby, journeyed to Scotland to glean first-hand knowledge concerning the reports of charismatic manifestations and healings. He observed the Macdonald family and their times of prayer and devotion, and was deeply impressed by their godly manner. Years later, he recorded his accounts in two books entitled *Memoirs of James and George Macdonald, of Port Glasgow* (1840), and *The Restoration of the Apostles and Prophets; in the Catholic Apostolic Church* (1861).

Thus, Norton became the self-appointed chronicler of Margaret's pretrib revelation, and carefully preserved her handwritten account in both of these books.

According to Norton's recollections, it was the first time anyone had divided the second coming into two distinct phases. A pertinent quote regarding Margaret's unique rapture revelation is as follows:

> Marvelous light was shed upon scripture, and especially on the doctrine of the second Advent, by the revived spirit of prophecy. In the following account by Miss M. Macdonald, of an evening during which the power of the Holy Ghost rested upon her for several successive hours, in mingled prophecy and vision, we have an instance; for here we first see the distinction between that final stage of the Lord's coming, when every eye shall see Him, and His prior appearing in glory to them that look for Him.[34]

In this statement Norton claims that she was the first individual to designate a distinction between a two-stage coming.

Norton then continues with Margaret's rambling prophetic revelation as follows:

> It was first the awful state of the land that was pressed upon me. I saw the blindness and infatuation of the people to be very great. I felt the

---

34. Robert Norton, *The Restoration of Apostles and Prophets; in the Catholic Apostolic Church*, p. 15.

cry of Liberty just to be the hiss of the serpent, to drown them in perdition. It was just "no God." I repeated the words, Now there is distress of nations, with perplexity, the seas and the waves roaring, men's hearts failing them for fear—now look out for the sign of the Son of man. Here I was made to stop and cry out, Oh it is now known what the sign of the Son of man is; the people of God think they are waiting, but they know not what it is. I felt this needed to be revealed, and that there was great darkness and error about it; but suddenly what it was burst upon me with a glorious light. I saw it was just the Lord himself descending from Heaven with a shout, just the glorified man, even Jesus; but that all must, as Stephen was, be filled with the Holy Ghost, that they might look up, and see the brightness of the Father's glory. I saw the error to be, that men think that it will be something seen by the natural eye; but 'tis spiritual discernment that is needed, the eye of God in his people. Many passages were revealed, in a light in which I had not before seen them. I repeated, "Now is the kingdom of Heaven like unto ten virgins, who went forth to meet the Bridegroom, five wise and five foolish; they that were foolish took their lamps, but took no oil with them; but they that were wise took oil in their vessels with their lamps." "But be ye not unwise, but understanding what the will of the Lord is; and be not drunk with wine wherein is excess, but be filled with the Spirit." This was the oil the wise virgins took in their vessels—this is the light to be kept burning—the light of God—that we may discern that which cometh not with observation to the natural eye. Only those who have the light of God within them will see the sign of his appearance. No need to follow them who say, see here, or see there, for his day shall be as the lightning to those in whom the living Christ is. 'Tis Christ in us that will lift us up—he is the light—'tis only those that are alive in him that will be caught up to meet him in the air. I saw that we must be in the Spirit, that we might see spiritual things. John was in the Spirit, when he saw a throne set in Heaven.—But I saw that the glory of the ministration of the Spirit had not been known. I repeated frequently, but the spiritual temple must and shall be reared, and the fulness of Christ be poured into his body, and then shall we be caught up to meet him. Oh none will be counted worthy of this calling but his body, which is the church, and which must be a candlestick all of gold. I often said, Oh the glorious temple which is now about to be reared, the bride adorned for her husband; and Oh what a holy, holy bride she must be, to be prepared for such a glorious bridegroom. I said, Now shall the people of God have to do with realities—now shall the glorious mystery of God in our nature be known—now shall it be known what it is for man to be glorified.

I felt that the revelation of Jesus Christ had yet to be opened up—it is not knowledge about God that it contains, but it is an entering into God—I saw that there was a glorious breaking in of God to be. I felt as Elijah, surrounded with chariots of fire. I saw as it were, the spiritual temple reared, and the Head Stone brought forth with shoutings of grace, grace unto it. It was a glorious light above the brightness of the sun, that shone round about me. I felt that those who were filled with the Spirit could see spiritual things, and be, as it were, walking in the midst of them, while those who had not the Spirit could see nothing—so that two shall be in one bed, the one taken and the other left, because the one has the light of God within while the other cannot see the kingdom of Heaven. I saw the people of God in an awfully dangerous situation, surrounded by nets and entanglements, about to be tried, and many about to be deceived and fall. Now will THE WICKED be revealed, with all power and signs and lying wonders, so that if it were possible the very elect will be deceived. This is the fiery trial which is to try us.—It will be for the purging and purifying of the real members of the body of Jesus; but Oh it will be a fiery trial. Every soul will be shaken to the very centre. The enemy will try to shake us in every thing we have believed—but the trial of real faith will be found to honour and praise and glory. Nothing but what is of God will stand. The stony-ground hearers will be made manifest—the love of many will wax cold. I frequently said that night, and often since, now shall the awful sight of a false Christ be seen on this earth, and nothing but the living Christ in us can detect this awful attempt of the enemy to deceive—for it is with all deceivableness of unrighteousness he will work—he will have a counterpart for every part of God's truth, and an imitation for every work of the Spirit. The Spirit must and will be poured out on the church, that she may be purified and filled with God—and just in proportion as the Spirit of God works, so will he—when our Lord anoints men with power, so will he. This is particularly the nature of the trial, through which those are to pass who will be counted worthy to stand before the Son of man. There will be outward trial, too, but 'tis principally temptation. It is brought on by the outpouring of the Spirit, and will just increase in proportion as the Spirit is poured out. The trial of the Church is from Antichrist. It is by being filled with the Spirit that we shall be kept. I frequently said, Oh be filled with the Spirit—have the light of God in you, that you may detect Satan—be filled with God. This will build the temple. It is not by might nor by power, but by my Spirit, saith the Lord. This will fit us to enter into the marriage supper of the Lamb. I saw it to be the will of God that all should be filled. But what hindered the real life of God from being received by his people, was their turning from Jesus, who is the way to the Father. They were not entering in by the door. For he is faithful who hath said, by me if any man enter in he shall find pasture. They were passing the cross, through which every drop of the Spirit of God flows to us. All power that comes not through the blood of Christ is not of God. When I say, they are looking from the cross, I feel that there is much in it—they turn from the blood of the Lamb, by which we overcome, and in which our robes are washed and made white. There are low views of God's holiness, and a ceasing to condemn sin in the flesh, and a looking from him who humbled himself, and made himself of no reputation. Oh! it is needed, much needed at present a leading back to the cross. I saw that night, and often since, that there will be an outpouring of the Spirit on the body, such as has not been, a baptism of fire, that all the dross may be put away. Oh there must and will be such an indwelling of the living God as has not been—the servants of God sealed in their foreheads—great conformity to Jesus—his holy, holy image seen in his people—just the bride made comely, by his comeliness put upon her. This is what we are at present made to pray much for, that speedily we may all be made ready to meet our Lord in the air—and it will be. Jesus wants his bride. His desire is toward us. He that shall come, will come, and will not tarry. Amen and Amen. Even so come Lord Jesus.[35]

Her handwritten account was also recorded by Norton in *The Restoration of the Apostles and Prophets; In the Catholic Apostolic Church* (1861).[36]

Margaret's handwritten revelation draws an important distinction between the final stage of Christ's coming when every eye shall behold Him, and a prior appearing for those who look for Him. She believed that only an exclusive company of believers would be raptured before the antichrist was revealed. But her vision specified that another company of believers would remain behind to endure the purifying pressures of the Great Tribulation. In essence, Margaret was not only the first pretribulation rapturist, but she was also the first partial rapturist.

Throughout the spring and summer months of 1830, Margaret's pretribulation perspective was being circulated among the many pocket

---

35. Robert Norton, *Memoirs of James and George Macdonald of Port Glasgow,* pp. 171-176.

36. Robert Norton, *The Restoration of the Apostles and Prophets; In the Catholic Apostolic Church,* pp. 15-18.

groups and prayer meetings being held in the surrounding towns of western Scotland. Her distinctive views were common knowledge to all those who visited her home. Both Darby and individuals from Irving's congregation were exposed to this novel teaching through contact with the Macdonald clan. It appears that both Irving and Darby borrowed from Margaret's original revelation. But, as I have previously indicated, Darby soon became the chief proponent.

While Darby quickly seized the opportunity to popularize this new teaching under his personal banner, he did slightly modify Margaret's position. Margaret believed in only a partial rapture of select Christians. Darby, on the other hand, kept the church intact and exempted them entirely from the terrors of the Great Tribulation. In short order, Darby expounded his borrowed pretrib views at the Powerscourt conferences and so vigorously and dogmatically promoted this prophetic innovation that it soon came to be looked upon as though it had always been the eternal truth of the scriptures.

The Growth of Pretribulationism

The almost evangelical spread of pretribulationism can be linked to the zealous efforts of John Darby. He was most responsible for introducing pretribulationism, along with a host of other innovations, into the mainstream of prophetic interpretation.

Whitby's postmillennialism, which down-played the importance of Christ's second coming, created a deep longing in the hearts of many for a more satisfying interpretation of prophecy. Darby catered to this hunger. His system of prophetic interpretation provided a fresh emphasis upon the doctrine of the second coming, and was enthusiastically embraced by multitudes, both in England and North America. Because of Darby's exhaustive efforts, pretribulationism, along with the entire system of dispensationalism, has become firmly rooted in the prophetic consciousness of millions today.

The Spiritual Pulse

An awareness of the spiritual condition of the early nineteenth century can help us comprehend the phenomenal spread of Darby's views. The church of the early 1800's was saturated with liberalism, orthodoxy, and lethargy. In some quarters, the doctrine of the second coming was actually ridiculed by the clergy. Sound doctrine was in short supply, and pulpits were often manned by professional clergy who seemed to care little for the spiritual welfare of the flock. Consequently, the average lay person was spiritually starving to death. It was in the midst of this confused theological climate that a growing desire for the clarion sound of truth was fostered. Against the backdrop of such spiritual dirth, it is little wonder that there was such a strong hunger for biblical truth and a fresh emphasis of hope.

Darby was the man of the hour. He stepped into this spiritual wasteland with a renewed message of expectancy, and stirred the church with a fresh emphasis upon prophecy and the second coming of Christ. His teachings satiated a deep longing in the hearts of many spiritually neglected people. Multitudes readily accepted his teachings in spite of his novelties in prophetic interpretation.

This is not surprising when we consider the spiritual climate of Darby's generation. As Cox commented:

> . . . We should not be surprised that Darbyism met with a ready response in such surroundings, neither should we be surprised if the people of that generation—with their lack of biblical teachings—passed all of Darby's spiritual "legislation" even though many of the bills in his legislation contained "riders" (strange innovations). Darby not only returned to the faith once delivered to the saints—which admittedly had been discarded and needed to be recovered—but he went far beyond that faith, bringing in many teachings of his own, which were never heard of until he brought them forth.[37]

To many, the good in Darby's system far outweighed the bad. His novel approach to prophetic inquiry was exceptionally appealing to many Christians, even if he did include certain modifications which were unheard of during previous church history. What mattered most was the fact that he exalted the glorious truth of Christ's second coming, and restored it to its rightful place of prominence. Ladd's comments at this juncture are helpful:

> . . . It is easy to see how Darbyian futurism possessed such attraction and impelling power. . . . His system of prophetic interpretation was eagerly adopted, not because of the attractiveness of the details of his system, but because its basic futurism seemed to be a recovery of a sound Biblical prophetic interpretation . . . and to give to the doctrine of the Lord's return the importance it deserved. In other words, Darbyism

---

37. William E. Cox, *An Examination of Dispensationalism,* p. 5.

to many Christians meant the rediscovery of the precious Biblical truth of Christ's glorious second coming, even though the basic truth was accompanied by some important details which were not essential to the premillennial return of Christ and which many later came to feel were not the Word of God.[38]

In spite of Darby's prophetic novelties, he, along with his Brethren compatriots, acted as a strong spiritual catalyst for the church. Their persuasions aside, they served as a beneficial stimulant for stirring an apathetic church out of their indifference and dead formalism. They vigorously challenged the widespread abuses and corruption, and promoted a long overdue interest in biblical study. Their chief error lies principally in their unusual prophetic concepts.

Darby was a prolific writer and traveled extensively. He toured the United States seven times between 1862 and 1877. During his travels to the States, he introduced his system of prophetic interpretation. For the most part, his views were enthusiastically accepted. In fact, though dispensationalism had originated in Europe, it made its greatest advances in North America where it is still firmly entrenched. His radical departure from traditional eschatological interpretation gained wide acceptance, sometimes even surmounting the formidable barriers of denominational creeds and challenges. This was largely due to the prophetic climate in America. During the mid-nineteenth century, the Christian community of America was undergoing a similar prophetic awakening. Darby's influence upon the prophetic scene helped give birth to the prophetic and Bible conference movement in America. Prophetic conferences, like their English counterparts before them, served as a platform for the further dissemination and popularization of pretribulational beliefs.

The Scofield Connection

Cyrus Ingerson Scofield (1843-1921) was born in Michigan, but grew up in Tennessee after his family moved there when he was a small boy. When the Civil War commenced in 1861, he joined the "Army of the Confederacy" and saw substantial combat during his enlistment. After the war, he entered the legal profession in St. Louis.

---

38. George E. Ladd, *The Blessed Hope*, p. 43.

Soon after his training, he became a practicing attorney in Washington D.C. During his budding law career in Washington, he gradually sank into alcoholism, but was eventually led to Christ through the determined efforts of another young lawyer in 1879. Three years later, he quit the legal profession to enter the ministry. In 1882 he assumed the pastorate of a small Congregational church in Dallas, Texas, where he spent the next thirteen years. In 1895, he was invited to become the pastor of the Congregational church in East Northfield, Massachusetts by the residing pastor, Dwight L. Moody. In 1902, he resigned his pastorate and returned to Dallas to devote his energies to the development of the now famous Scofield Reference Bible.

Many influential leaders followed Darby's lead. But the single greatest factor in the propagation of pretribulationism can be traced to the efforts of Scofield. Darby's entire system of prophetic futurism owes much of its success and establishment to the efforts of Scofield. Scofield was quite taken with Darby's perspective and became an ardent supporter. He had been studiously absorbed by Darby's teachings for years. He whole-heartedly embraced Darby's eschatological system, and eventually included his ideas in the Scofield Reference Bible which was published in 1909. It has sold over three million copies since its publication, and has exerted a tremendous influence upon the prophetic consciousness of many. As Pieters asserted, "It may fairly be called one of the most influential books—perhaps it is the most influential single work—thrust into the religious life of America during the twentieth century."[39] It has become, in effect, the standard textbook of all dispensational persuasions, and is the primary source of biblical commentary for thousands.

Scofield utilized the King James Version, and incorporated his own explanatory notes. This was revolutionary, and in direct conflict with the long established policies of the well known Bible societies whose strict motto was, "Without note or comment." To many people, Scofield's ideas have been granted equality with the divinely inspired Word of God. The inclusion of his explanatory notes alongside of scripture gave his comments a subtle legitimacy which has quietly affected many—even when his views were faulty. To many an unsuspecting student, the Scofield Reference Bible has actually been responsible for undermining the clarity of God's Word. As Mauro

---

39. Albertus Pieters, *The Scofield Bible*, p. 4.

asserted, ". . . the Scofield Bible . . . (which is the main vehicle of the new system of doctrine referred to [dispensationalism - mine]) has usurped the place of authority that belongs to God's Bible alone."[40]

Though his notes are basically sound as far as the cardinal doctrines of Christianity are concerned, his comments on prophecy are an embodiment of the faulty exegesis employed by Darby in the formulation of his system of prophetic interpretation. In fact, many of Scofield's comments are in direct conflict with the historic teaching of the Christian church. At times, the Scofield Bible even questions the reliability of some of the teachings embraced by historic Christianity. He often does so with such a dogmatic air of finality that one wonders whether any opposing viewpoint could contain an ounce of credibility.

Another book which helped fan the flames of pretribulationism and dispensational theology was William E. Blackstone's *Jesus Is Coming* (1878). This book has been translated into many languages, and hundreds of thousands of copies have been distributed worldwide. This work has been instrumental in helping popularize a pretrib rapture, and stands only behind Scofield's Bible in doing so. Another book by James H. Brooks entitled, *Maranatha, or the Lord Cometh* (1870) was also influential in promoting this concept.

Other significant contributors to the rise and spread of pretribulationism include William Kelley, Charles H. Mackintosh, A. T. Pierson, J. M. Gray, R. A. Torrey, Charles Feinberg, Arno C. Gaebelein, Charles Stanley, Lewis Sperry Chafer, E. W. Bullinger, H. A. Ironside, Richard DeHaan, Charles Ryrie, Dwight Pentecost, Oral Roberts, Carl McIntire, Billy Graham, John Walvoord, W. A. Criswell, Hal Lindsey, Tim LaHaye, and Jerry Falwell. These key individuals, along with a host of others, have helped perpetuate the spread of pretribulationism and dispensational teachings over the last 150 years.

Distinguished Pretrib Opponents

In spite of the fact that pretribulationists can rally many notable individuals to their position, there is a distinguished array of renowned Christians who do not support a pretribulation rapture theory. Some of the outstanding Christian leaders who never embraced this teaching or who initially embraced it only to eventually renounce it include:

---

40. Philip Mauro, *The Gospel of the Kingdom,* p. 5.

Henry Alford, Oswald T. Allis, Matthew Arnold, David Baren, J. Sidlow
Baxter, Dr. Bergin, Louis Berkhof, Rowland V. Bingham, Del Birkey,
Lorraine Boettner, Dr. Horatius Bonar, William Booth, F. F. Bruce,
John Bunyan, Herbert W. Butt, John Calvin, Robert Cameron,
Edward J. Carnell, Thomas Chalmers, Adam Clarke, Harry Conn,
Dr. Charles T. Cook, Samuel Cooper, John Cotton, Alexander Cruden,
Franz Delitzsch, Jonathan Edwards, Charles R. Erdman, W. J. Erdman,
Howard Ferrin, Charles Finney, Paul B. Fischer, John Foxe, Alexander
Fraser, George H. Fromow, LeRoy Froom, Henry W. Frost, John
Gill, A. J. Gordon, Jack Green, H. Grattan Guiness, Robert H. Gundry,
Roy E. Hayden, William Hendriksen, Carl F. H. Henry, Matthew
Henry, Herschel H. Hobbs, Charles Hodge, Bishop Frank Houghton,
Thomas Houghton, Henry T. Hudson, John Huss, Orson Jones,
Russell B. Jones, Arthur D. Katterjohn, John Knox, H. L. Lindsay-
Young, C. S. Lovett, William G. Lowe, Martin Luther, J. Gresham
Machen, Norman S. MacPherson, Cotton Mather, Philip Mauro, S. I.
McMillen, Robert E. McNeill, Robert C. McQuilkin, Philipp Melancthon,
Dale Moody, Dr. Campbell Morgan, W. G. Moorehead, Leon Morris,
E. Y. Mullens, George Muller, Iain H. Murray, Augustus Neander,
Isaac Newton, Thomas Newton, Dr. Harold J. Ockenga, Eric C.
Peters, A. W. Pink, Bernard Ramm, Alexander Reese, Harry Rimmer,
William J. Rowlands, R. J. Rushdoony, Dr. Adolph Saphir, Ed. F.
Sanders, Dr. A. B. Simpson, Oswald J. Smith, H. W. Soltau, Charles
W. Spurgeon, A. H. Strong, Dr. J. W. Thirtle, S. P. Tregelles, William
Tyndale, Henry Varley, B. B. Warfield, John Wesley, Dr. Nathaniel
West, Frank H. White, George Whitefield, Robert Dick Wilson, Robert
Young, Robert F. Youngblood, and Theodor Zahn.

This impressive list of Christian leaders may be quite sobering to
many who were under the mistaken impression that modern pretribulationism has been a foundational truth enthusiastically embraced
and defended by most of the great Christian scholars. What is more,
some of the most vocal critics of pretribulationism are individuals
who defected from their camp (myself included).

Furthermore, it should be stated that none of the great creeds or
confessions give mention or support to the concept of a pretribulation
rapture. Neither "The Apostles' Creed," "The Nicene Creed," "The
Athanasian Creed," "The Westminster Confession of Faith," "The
Savoy Declaration," "The Baptist Confession of 1689," "The
Philadelphia Confession of Faith," "The Morland Confession of 1508
and 1535," "The Helvetic Confession," "The Belgic Confession,"

"The Augsbury Confession," or "The Smalkald Article" of the Lutheran church defend this theory.

The Bottom Line

In reviewing the issue of historic authenticity, we have seen that the pretribulation rapture theory is a comparatively recent innovation in prophetic interpretation. History conclusively demonstrates that it was not an eschatological position embraced by the church at any point prior to the 1830's. Neither has the claim been substantiated that it is a refinement or recovery of those cherished beliefs taught during the apostolic or post-apostolic era. Its earliest origins are deeply rooted in the "Prophetic Awakening" of the early nineteenth century. It was basically an outgrowth of the heightened interest in prophetic inquiry and the redefining of prophetic perspectives which emerged during this period in church history.

In conclusion, it is only fair to add the observation that the historic origin of an interpretation of scripture is not an absolute measure of accuracy. I have appealed to the issue of historic authenticity to establish an understanding of the developments in eschatological interpretation. In doing so, I have shown that pretribulationists' claims that this theory has always been a sacred teaching since apostolic times is unwarranted and unjustifiable. However, in the final analysis, I recognize that the ultimate touchstone in determining the validity of any doctrinal perspective is the Word of God.

In the remaining chapters we will consider the scriptural validity of pretribulationism. We will do so by a point-by-counter point appraisal of the common areas of controversy surrounding this subject. In so doing, I will further demonstrate that this teaching is not a legitimate biblical concept, and that the preponderance of scriptural evidence against it is overwhelming.

3

The Rapture—Secret & Silent?

Though all genuine Christians accept the scriptural validity of the "catching-up" of the saints as depicted in I Thessalonians 4:17, the question of exact timing continues to create controversy. In debating the issue of timing, several common arguments have arisen. In the following chapters we will carefully consider the merits of these familiar areas of controversy in order to determine whether or not the scriptures substantiate the concept of a pretrib rapture.

One of the most frequent areas of disagreement focuses upon the characteristics of the rapture. One of the commonly heard contentions of pretrib advocates is that the rapture will be secret, silent, and mysterious. The idea that Christ will come suddenly and silently to secretly snatch away His waiting bride for a heavenly elopement of seven years before returning to earth is a belief which is endorsed by millions of contemporary Christians. Such descriptive comings as,

. . . in the rapture, only the Christians see Him—it's a mystery, a secret. When the living believers are taken out, the world is going to be mystified.[1]

Quickly and invisibly, unperceived by the world, the Lord will come as a thief in the night and catch away His waiting saints.[2]

His appearance in the clouds will be veiled to the human eye and no one will see Him. He will slip in, slip out; move in to get His jewels, and slip out as under the cover of night.[3]

. . . the word of God tells us that the Second Coming of Christ, his appearing for his saints . . . is a secret Rapture! In all the earth . . . only a handful of saints will know that Christ has returned for his Bride and then left again.[4]

An Appeal to Sensationalism

Proponents of a secret pretrib rapture frequently appeal to sensationalism in order to promote their position. They often depict dramatic post-rapture scenarios in order to captivate the attention of both the secular and Christian public. As Boettner commented:

The doctrine of an any moment Rapture, and particularly that of a secret Rapture, lends itself to the dramatic and the sensational. In treating this subject, on which even its proponents can find but little revealed in scripture, the human mind can give full reign to its imaginative powers. The event is supposed to occur in absolute secrecy. Consternation and confusion reign among those who are left behind when they wake up to discover that all the Christians have suddenly vanished. Bewilderment and terrifying scenes follow as families are separated and all the best neighbors are gone. They search everywhere, but cannot find them. Industries and utilities are immobilized. Hearts are filled with fear and dread.[5]

The following quotes are representative of such sensationalized accounts:

Imagine getting up some morning and your wife is not there, and you call for her, but there is no answer. You go downstairs, but she is not

1. Hal Lindsey, *The Late Great Planet Earth,* p. 131.
2. Jesse F. Silver, *The Lord's Return,* p. 200.
3. Oral Roberts, *How To Be Personally Prepared for the Second Coming of Christ,* p. 34.
4. Lloyd L. Goodwin, *The Three Comings of Our Lord Jesus Christ,* p. 22.
5. Lorraine Boettner, *The Millennium,* p. 172.

there. You call upstairs to daughter asking where mother is, but no answer from daughter. Daughter too is gone. You ring the police but the line is busy. Hundreds and thousands are calling up, jamming the telephone lines. You rush out of doors and bump into the pal of last night's wild party. He is white as a sheet. He is out of breath, and he stammers a few words, and bawls out, "My wife is gone. My brother is gone, and I don't know where they are." Down the streets runs a woman shrieking at the top of her voice, "Someone has kidnapped my baby!" and in a moment the streets are full of people, weeping, crying and howling over the disappearance of loved ones. What has happened? The Lord has come, like a thief in the night. He has quietly stolen away those who trusted him, like Enoch, and no one is left behind to warn you any more, to pray or show you the way.[6]

Another classic example is as follows:

When Christ comes the invisible Church will be caught up out of the midst of the visible. It will be a secret rapture—quiet, noiseless, sudden as the step of a thief in the night. All that the world will know will be that multitudes at once have gone. The extras will advertise in the streets, "Universal Consternation—Remarkable Disappearances." Such and such ministers are missing. Such and such business men are not to be found. Such and such women of high and low position have left their places vacant. The next Sunday the fashionable churches will show certain of their seats empty. In smaller, more devout churches, the majority will be gone—only a remnant left. For some days nothing else can be talked about. Excitement will be tremendous. Then reaction will set in. Philosophers and rationalistic ministers will begin to account for the phenomenon on scientific principles. The world will resume its occupations. Gradually the breaches in the churches will be closed up. Only a few here and there will wake up and say, "It is too late! I am left out. My godly relatives have gone—the Spirit of God has departed. The reign of evil has begun. We have slept away our day of grace!"[7]

These and similar characterizations are repeatedly echoed through the electronic media, reinforced through pretribulational literature, distributed through Christian films, and even advertised through bumper sticker graffiti.

---

6. Richard W. DeHaan, *Radio Bible Class,* Nov. 1954.
7. George Sayles Bishop, *The Doctrines of Grace,* p. 341.

However, many students of biblical prophecy challenge such sensationalized characterizations on the grounds that they can find no credible support in the scriptures.

> The Bible knows nothing about a secret coming of Christ or of His catching up of His people in a kind of elopement in which only those called away will be involved. All the sensational horror stories about pilots secretly leaving their planes in the air, doctors mysteriously disappearing from operating rooms, children being wafted away as by evaporation from mothers' arms, and dictaphones running on with no secretaries to transcribe, are lying figments of human imaginations, that have absolutely no foundation or support in God's revealed truth.[8]

Not only do many posttribulationists find the notion of a secret rapture inconsistent with the testimony of scripture, but it should also be clarified that many pretribulationists quietly ignore this point altogether. They remain conveniently uncommitted and noticeably silent regarding the issue of a silent, mysterious rapture. But this reaction is not particularly surprising when considered against the backdrop of the actual scriptural characterization of this event!

How Secret Is Secret?

To settle the issue of whether or not there will be a secret, silent rapture, we must examine those scriptures pertaining to this event. The most important passage is I Thessalonians 4:13-17. This is the so-called "Magna Carta" of pretribulational teaching, and is often appealed to by advocates of this perspective. As Walvoord noted, "Probably more pretribulationists base their conclusion for a pretribulation rapture on I Thessalonians 4 than on any other single passage of scripture."[9]

> But I would not have you to be ignorant, brethren, concerning them which are asleep, that ye sorrow not, even as others which have no hope. For if we believe that Jesus died and rose again, even so them also which sleep in Jesus will God bring with him. For this we say unto you by the word of the Lord, that we which are alive and remain unto the coming of the Lord shall not prevent them which are asleep. For the Lord himself shall descend from heaven with a shout, with the voice of the

8. *The Researcher,* Fall, 1982, Vol. 12, No. 3, p. 12.
9. John F. Walvoord, *The Blessed Hope and the Tribulation,* p. 94.

archangel, and with the trump of God: and the dead in Christ shall rise first: Then we which are alive and remain shall be caught up together with them in the clouds, to meet the Lord in the air: and so shall we ever be with the Lord (I Thess. 4:13-17).

Even a cursory glance at this pivotal rapture text dispels the notion of a secret rapture. As one author noted:

> There is nothing in scripture to suggest that the dead will rise amid a great silence . . . surely you will not say that the trumpet, by any stretch of the imagination, can be intended to mean some secret procedure. The very idea of "the shout," "the voice of the archangel," and the "trump of God" proclaim an audible, public event. I cannot find, then, in this specific scripture (I Thess. 4:13-18) any authority for the secret Rapture of the saints. I am myself persuaded that there is not one shred of scripture anywhere to support this theory. I am sure that it is a figment of human imagination.[10]

In commenting upon this crucial rapture passage, Alexander Reese, one of this century's most notable opponents of pretribulationism, voiced his outrage at this teaching as follows:

> The suggestions of Darby . . . and others, to prove from this magnificent passage in I Thessalonians 4, that a secret coming, a resurrection, and a secret rapture are supported . . . is among the sorriest in the whole history of freak exegesis . . . It is as pure a myth as ever entered the brain of man.[11]

Though this language is a bit caustic, his comments do reflect the sentiments of many towards the concept of a secret rapture theory.

The obvious implication of this key verse is that the rapture will be anything but a quiet, secret event. Such words as "shout," "voice," and "trump of God" indicate that the rapture will be a noisy, open, and spectacular event. I Thessalonians 4:16, 17 is not a subtle description of a hidden, silent event, but something that will be loud, patent, and spectacular! As someone jokingly commented, "Unless we take the trump of God to be a dog whistle and interpret the shout of Christ and the voice of the archangel to be performed with sign language, the rapture will be quite conspicuous!" "Surely this . . . verse is a

---

10. T. T. Sheilds, *The Gospel Witness,* Sept. 21, 1935.
11. Alexander Reese, *The Approaching Advent of Christ,* pp. 146, 148.

strange one on which to found a doctrine of a secret rapture! It would seem rather to be just about the noisiest verse in the entire Bible!"[12] Fletcher added, "If anyone can make a secret coming out of this scripture, language has no significance at all."[13]

One must wonder how Paul could conceivably have written these verses pertaining to the rapture (something to which all pretribulationists agree) if he had in mind the thought of a secret rapture. The descriptive language which he employs within these passages is particularly vivid and meaningful. It argues forcefully against a clandestine coming. For example, when commenting upon the Greek word translated "shout," Morris stated,

> The "shout" denotes an authoritative utterance. The word is found quite often. It is the cry made by the ship's master to his rower, or by a military officer to his soldiers, or by a hunter to his hounds, or by a charioteer to his horses. When used to military or naval personnel, it was a battle cry. In most places, then, it denotes a loud authoritative cry, often one uttered in the thick of great excitement. All those associations make it an apt word for the great day to which Paul looked forward.[14]

In his graphic exposition of I Thessalonians 4:13-18, Kretzmann completely undermines the notion of a secret rapture with this dramatic depiction:

> . . . the Lord Himself, the exalted Christ, will appear in the clouds of heaven, visible, as He ascended upon high. With great power and might He will come down from heaven, Acts 1:11, with a loud summons, with a shout of command, as a victorious captain going forth to the destruction of His enemies, with the voice of an archangel summoning the great host of heavenly spirits, with a trumpet of God, a majestic note that will strike terror into the hearts of His enemies and cause the hearts of believers to beat higher with exultant joy, the great King will descend from His throne. It will be, as Luther writes, like the coming of a great and powerful king or emperor in full battle array, filling the air with

---

12. Lorraine Boettner, *The Millennium,* p. 171.
13. George B. Fletcher, *Will a Secret Rapture Precede the Second Coming of Christ?* p. 3.
14. Leon Morris, *The New International Commentary, I & II Thessalonians,* p. 143.

the clamor of battle-cries and trumpets. The shouting of the victorious conqueror of death and hell will reach the dead in their graves, the believers will hear the voice of their Savior, and they will come forth from their graves with glorified bodies, ready to join Him in His triumphal pageant.[15]

When we honestly examine the descriptive nature and tone of these key rapture passages, it is quite obvious why pretrib advocates are so hard pressed to defend the concept of a secret, silent rapture. However, even in the face of such a glaring characterization, these verses are repeatedly used as supposed "proof texts" for material which depicts the rapture as a secret, hidden, and quiet coming of Christ.

"A Thief in the Night"

Pretribulationists sometimes appeal to those scriptures which teach that the Lord will come as a "thief in the night." They contend that the so-called "thief" passages give credence to the concept of a secret rapture. They interpret these passages to mean that the Lord's coming for His saints will be a secret and silent event in which He will imperceptibly and mysteriously snatch the believers out of this world so that the remainder of humanity will be at a total loss to explain their mysterious disappearance. As far as a bewildered humanity is concerned, the case of the "missing millions" will be the greatest unsolved kidnapping in history!

The figurative expressions employed by Jesus, Paul, Peter, and John to liken the characteristics of the Lord's coming for His saints to that of a thief were never intended to convey the idea that the Lord will prowl around like a thief, acting in stealth, operating under the cover of darkness. As Woodrow stated, "The meaning is that Christ will return as a thief, not that he will act like a thief!"[16] His coming as a thief simply means that it will be sudden, unannounced, and unexpected—not that it will be silent and sneaky. His coming will be a complete surprise to all those who are not waiting and watching

---

15. Paul E. Kretzmann, *Popular Commentary of the Bible, New Testament, Vol. II,* p. 353.
16. Ralph Woodrow, *Great Prophecies of the Bible,* p. 9.

for His blessed appearing. The rapture will not be a covert operation. The following prophetic passages compare the Lord's return to a thief:

> But know this, that if the goodman of the house had known in what watch the *thief* would come, he would have watched, and would not have suffered his house to be broken up. Therefore be ye also ready: for in an hour as ye think not the Son of man cometh (Matt. 24:43, 44; see also Luke 12:39, 40).

> For yourselves know perfectly that the day of the Lord so cometh as a *thief* in the night (I Thess. 5:2).

> But ye, brethren, are not in darkness, that that day should overtake you as a *thief* (I Thess. 5:4).

> But the day of the Lord will come as a *thief* in the night; in the which the heavens shall pass away with a great noise, and the elements shall melt with fervent heat, the earth also and the works that are therein shall be burned up (II Peter 3:10).

> Remember therefore how thou hast received and heard, and hold fast, and repent. If therefore thou shalt not watch, I will come on thee as a *thief*, and thou shalt not know what hour I will come upon thee (Rev. 3:3).

> Behold, I come as a *thief*. Blessed is he that watcheth, and keepeth his garments, lest he walk naked, and they see his shame (Rev. 16:15).

The intended thrust of all of these passages is to alert Christendom to the urgent necessity of remaining spiritually awake, alert, and watchful because of the unexpected timing surrounding the Lord's coming for His saints. But they do not subtly imply that His coming will be silent and hidden. For example, in Christ's parable of "the thief in the night" we read:

> But know this, that if the goodman of the house had known in what watch the thief would come, he would have watched, and would not have suffered his house to be broken up. Therefore be ye also ready: for in such an hour as ye think not the Son of man cometh (Matt. 24:43, 44; see also Luke 12:39, 40).

> In Matthew's parable of "the thief in the night" . . . the Lord emphasizes the pressing need for constant watchfulness by comparing the uncertainty of the timing of His return to the unsuspecting approach of

a thief in the night. The obvious point is that His disciples must not conduct themselves as the unprepared householder who foolishly permitted his house to be broken into because he failed to recognize the reality that thieves do not brazenly advertise beforehand the timing of their arrival.[17]

Christ's obvious implication is that He will return like a thief in the sense that we will not know precisely when the second coming will occur. Therefore, we have been entrusted with the responsibility of remaining watchful at all seasons. However, there is nothing contained in this parable to indicate that the event itself will be secret. In parallel manner, the "thief" passages of Revelation 3:3 and 16:15 are also intended to caution the Christian community to preparedness and vigilance rather than subtly conveying the idea of the secret, mysterious nature of His coming.

In examining the other "thief" passages in light of their scriptural context, we find that, contrary to the pretribulationists' assertion, the rapture will be anything but secret and silent. For example, I Thessalonians 5:1, 2 is found in direct context with the noted rapture passage of I Thessalonians 4:16, 17, in which the Lord's coming is accompanied with a "shout," "the voice of the archangel," and the "trump of God." Paul continues on in the immediate context of chapter 5 to declare that the saints knew "perfectly that the day of the Lord so cometh AS A THIEF IN THE NIGHT" (I Thess. 5:2). Linking this statement to the previous information given in the context of chapter 4, we find that His coming will be glorious, open, and noisy! What is more, Paul continues with these words:

> For when they shall say, Peace and safety; then SUDDEN DESTRUCTION cometh upon them, as travail upon a woman with child; and they shall not escape. But ye, brethren, are not in darkness, that that day [the day when He comes as a thief] should overtake you as a thief (1 Thess. 5:3, 4).

The clear contextual implications of these verses is that the Lord's coming as a "thief" will be a day accompanied with sudden destruction being unleashed upon those who dwell in darkness, and not a silent, unobserved, mysterious disappearance of millions of people from the planet earth, as some speculators would have us believe.

---

17. William H. Kimball, *What the Bible Says About the Great Tribulation*, p. 242.

The final "thief" passage is found in II Peter 3:10. This verse is found in the context of a chapter which is entirely eschatological in nature. Peter informs his readers that "there shall come in the last days scoffers, walking after their own lusts, and saying 'Where is the promise of his coming?'" (II Peter 3:3, 4). He then assures his readers that "the day of the Lord will come as a THIEF IN THE NIGHT" (II Peter 3:10). But Peter doesn't stop there. He continues to inform them that the Lord's coming as a thief will not be quiet, but cataclysmic, "in the which the heavens shall pass away with GREAT NOISE, and the elements shall melt with fervent heat, the earth also and the works that are therein shall be burned up" (II Peter 3:10). The graphic wording lends absolutely no support to the supposed secret nature of this thief passage. Surely Peter would not have employed the descriptive wording "great noise" or couple such a catastrophic event as "the heavens" passing "away," the elements melting "with fervent heat," or the earth and the works therein being "burned up" if he had intended this "thief" passage to be taken in a silent context.

In view of the clear teaching of God's Word, we can find no viable, scriptural defense to substantiate the assumption that the rapture will be a secret, invisible, and quiet event. As Murray bluntly concluded, "There is no plain teaching in the Bible to show that the church of God will be raptured secretly, but much plain teaching to the contrary."[18] Contrary to the obvious contexts associated with the thief passages, we still have prophetic leaders declaring that the rapture will be silent and unnoticed by the world.

Selected Scriptures

Apart from these "thief" passages, several other outstanding second coming scriptures undermine the concept of a secret, silent rapture. Each supports the position that the rapture event will be audible, visible, and public.

For example, in II Thessalonians 1:7-10 we read:

> And to you who are troubled rest with us, when the Lord Jesus shall be revealed from heaven with his mighty angels, in flaming fire taking

---

18. George L. Murray, *Millennial Studies,* p. 142.

vengeance on them that know not God, and that obey not the gospel of our Lord Jesus Christ: Who shall be punished with everlasting destruction from the presence of the Lord, and from the glory of his power: When he shall come to be glorified in his saints, and to be admired in all them that believe (because our testimony among you was believed) in that day.

Even a casual examination of these verses reveals that the coming of Christ "to be glorified in his saints" is synonymous with His coming "from heaven with his mighty angels, in flaming fire taking vengeance on them that know not God and that obey not the gospel of our Lord Jesus Christ." These verses clearly reveal that Christ's return for His saints directly coincides with the timing when He shall unleash His awesome judgments upon an unbelieving world. These verses demonstrate that the reward of the righteous and the punishment of the wicked are intimately inter-woven. Obviously, such vivid language can not, by any stretch of the imagination, be interpreted in a silent, secret context. Such phrases as "revealed from heaven with his mighty angels," "in flaming fire taking vengeance," and "punished with everlasting destruction from the presence of the Lord" argue forcefully against the pretribulational notion of a secret rapture.

The Mount Olivet prophecy includes several key passages which characterize the second coming:

For as the lightning cometh out of the east, and shineth even unto the west: so shall also the coming of the Son of man be (Matt. 24:27).

And then shall appear the sign of the Son of man in heaven: and then shall all the tribes of the earth mourn, and they shall see the Son of man coming in the clouds of heaven with power and great glory. And he shall send his angels with a great sound of a trumpet, and they shall gather together his elect from the four winds, from one end of heaven to the other (Matt. 24:30, 31).

But as the days of Noe were, so shall also the coming of the Son of man be. For as in the days that were before the flood they were eating and drinking, marrying and giving in marriage, until the day that Noe entered into the ark, and knew not until the flood came, and took them all away; so shall also the coming of the Son of man be (Matt. 24:37-39).

Each of these passages refute the concept of a secret, silent coming of Christ for His saints. In Matthew 24:27, His coming is likened unto a bolt of lightning. It will be visible, audible, and spectacular. In

Matthew 24:30, 31, Christ's return is accompanied with His "coming in the clouds of heaven with power and great glory," with "his angels," with the "GREAT SOUND of a trumpet," and with the gathering of "his elect" from the far corners of the earth. Again, the descriptive wording lends absolutely no support to a secret rapture.

Finally, Christ compared His return to the days of Noah. On the "same day" that the deluge was unleashed upon a corrupt humanity, Noah and his family were delivered. Jesus affirmed that they ". . . knew not until the flood came, and took them all away; so shall also the coming of the Son of man be" (Matt. 24:39). In commenting upon these verses, Woodrow offered this perceptive statement: "The wicked knew not until the flood came—but, obviously, when it came they knew it. It was no secret event. It was observed by believers and unbelievers."[19] Obviously, the deluge was not a secret, mass drowning in conjunction with Noah's rescue.

The same points could be made of Luke's comparison of Christ's second coming to the days of Lot (Luke 17:28-30). Jesus plainly stated that, "The SAME DAY that Lot went out of Sodom it rained fire and brimstone from heaven, and destroyed them all." He concluded by declaring that, "Even thus shall it be IN THE DAY WHEN THE SON OF MAN IS REVEALED." Clearly, these verses demonstrate that the timing of God's deliverance for His people coincides with the execution of His judgments upon the ungodly. Obviously, He was not suggesting a secret judgment or deliverance. An honest interpretation of these prophetic passages shows that Christ's return will be quite conspicuous.

Several other selected passages further disprove the dispensationalists' notion of a secret rapture. For example, in Revelation 1:7 and Acts 1:11 we read:

> Behold, he cometh with clouds; and every eye shall see him, and they also which pierced him: and all kindreds of the earth shall wail because of him (Rev. 1:7).

> Which also said, Ye men of Galilee, why stand ye gazing up into heaven? this same Jesus, which is taken up from you into heaven, shall so come in like manner as ye have seen him go into heaven (Acts 1:11).

---

19. Ralph Woodrow, *Great Prophecies of the Bible*, p. 9.

66

Both of these companion verses reveal that Christ's return will be very conspicuous. Each affirm that He will come in the clouds. This fact is in harmony with other New Testament passages which associate His coming with clouds such as I Thessalonians 4:16, 17 (see also Matt. 24:30). They each suggest that His return will be clearly visible to the naked eye. Revelation 1:7 even goes so far as to state that, "EVERY EYE SHALL SEE HIM." Surely, these verses lend little support to a secret rapture.

Another key rapture passage is recorded in I Corinthians:

> Behold, I shew you a mystery; We shall not all sleep, but we shall all be changed, in a moment, in the twinkling of an eye, at the last trump: for the trumpet shall sound, and the dead shall be raised incorruptible, and we shall be changed" (I Cor. 15:51, 52).

This verse parallels the same descriptive wording used in I Thessalonians 4:13-18. It should be stressed that the phrase "the trumpet shall sound" does not uphold a silent rapture theory, unless of course its a secret "sounding."

In closing, the pretribulational treatment of these verses, in attempting to substantiate the notion of a secret rapture, does little interpretive justice to their intended meaning. A candid review of the selected second coming passages which we have covered proves that none can be used to enforce the concept of a secret, silent rapture.

These scriptures, along with a multitude of others which we will examine in the course of this study, form an avalanche of truth against this perspective. We will demonstrate that pretribulationism is often a doctrinal quagmire, much like quicksand. The more earnestly its advocates struggle to free themselves from its internal inconsistencies and errors, the deeper they sink into the mire of Biblical confusion and contradiction.

4

Wrath, Tribulation, or Rapture?

One of the widely used arguments of pretribulationists to bolster their position is the assumption that, since the Great Tribulation will be a period which will involve the unparalleled outpouring of God's wrath upon the world, it would be inconceivable to imagine God permitting His church to remain upon the earth and suffer from the awesome terrors and judgment of a great, global tribulation along with a corrupt and unregenerate humanity. This is a popular position of pretrib supporters and can be found in the writings of most pretribulationists. For example, Walvoord, one of the most ardent advocates of pretribulationism, inquired,

> Why should a child of God's grace—who is saved by grace, who is kept by grace, who has all the wonderful promises of God—be forced to go through a period which, according to scripture, is expressly designed as a time of judgment upon a Christ-rejecting world?[1]

1. John F. Walvoord, *The Thessalonican Epistles*, p. 83.

Defenders of a pretrib rapture point to several supposed "proof texts" in order to prove the church's exemption from wrath and tribulation:

> Verily, verily, I say unto you, He that heareth my word, and believeth on him that sent me, hath everlasting life, and shall not come into condemnation; but is passed from death unto life (John 5:24).

> Much more then, being now justified by his blood, we shall be saved from wrath through him (Rom. 5:9).

> There is therefore now no condemnation to them which are in Christ Jesus, who walk not after the flesh, but after the Spirit (Rom. 8:1).

> And to wait for his Son from heaven, whom he raised from the dead, even Jesus, which delivered us from the wrath to come (I Thess. 1:10).

> Forbidding us to speak to the Gentiles that they might be saved, to fill up their sins alway: for the wrath is come upon them to the uttermost (I Thess. 2:16).

> For God hath not appointed us to wrath, but to obtain salvation by our Lord Jesus Christ (I Thess. 5:9).

Two other pertinent passages pointed to by pretribulationists are Luke 21:36 and Revelation 3:10. We will review these separately in the course of this chapter.

On the surface, this popular pretrib position seems persuasive. However, a thorough examination of the relevant New Testament passages reveals that this argument contains only superficial logic at best. What is more, the bottom line thrust of this position is that it is presented in such a manner as to appeal to the fear factor rather than a rightly dividing of God's Word.

God's Wrath

The scriptures clearly teach us that the church will never suffer from the wrath of God. There will be no "spill-over" effect. This point is agreed upon by all, whether they are pre or posttribulationists. It is inconceivable to imagine the church suffering from the direct wrath of God, whether it involves an extended period of divine judgment commonly referred to as The Great Tribulation, or a final burst of destructive fury unleashed against the world in immediate conjunction with the timing of the second coming (see II Thess. 1:7-9 and Rev. 19:11-21). This is a perverted concept akin to depicting Christ as a masochist who inflicts unwarranted punishments upon His own body.

The scriptures clearly assure those who have been redeemed by the blood of the Lamb that they are unconditionally delivered from the wrath of God. A number of key passages confirm this assurance:

He that believeth on the Son hath everlasting life: and he that believeth not the Son shall not see life; but the wrath of God abideth on him (John 3:36).

For the wrath of God is revealed from heaven against all ungodliness and unrighteousness of men, who hold the truth in unrighteousness (Rom. 1:18).

But after thy hardness and impenitent heart treasurest up unto thy self wrath against the day of wrath and revelation of the righteous judgment of God (Rom. 2:5).

Much more then, being now justified by his blood, we shall be saved from wrath through him (Rom. 5:9).

Among whom also we all had our conversation in times past in the lusts of our flesh . . . and of the mind; and were by nature the children of wrath, even as others (Eph. 2:3).

Let no man deceive you with vain words: for because of these things cometh the wrath of God upon the children of disobedience (Eph. 5:6).

And to wait for his Son from heaven, whom he raised from the dead, even Jesus, which delivered us from the wrath to come (I Thess. 1:10).

For God hath not appointed us to wrath, but to obtain salvation by our Lord Jesus Christ (I Thess. 5:9).

In flaming fire taking vengeance on them that know not God, and that obey not the gospel of our Lord Jesus Christ (II Thess. 1:8).

These verses reveal that God's wrath only resides upon those who refuse to embrace Jesus Christ as Lord (John 3:36); that *"the wrath of God is revealed from heaven against all ungodliness and unrighteousness of men, who hold the truth in unrighteousness"* (Rom. 1:18); that the impenitent and obstinate are storing up the wrath of God which will be revealed on *"the day of wrath and revelation of the righteousness judgment of God"* (Rom. 2:5); that those that are *"justified by his blood . . . shall be saved from wrath through him"* (Rom. 5:9); that before our conversion we were characterized as *"the children of wrath"* (Eph. 2:2); that the *"wrath of God"* will come *"upon the children of disobedience"* (Eph. 5:6); that we are *"delivered . . . from the wrath to come"* (I Thess. 1:10); and that when Christ returns, He will take *"vengeance on them that know not God,*

71

and . . . obey not the gospel of our Lord Jesus Christ: who shall be punished with everlasting destruction from the presence of the Lord . . ." (II Thess. 1:8, 9). All of these passages clearly prove that God's people are immune from His wrath.

The frequently heard argument that the church must be evacuated from the earth in order to escape the consequences of the outpouring of God's wrath during a period of great tribulation is based upon the simplistic premise that, since God's wrath is clearly not intended for Christians, it stands to reason that Christians will not be upon the earth when God's wrath is unleashed!

However, posttribulationists can point to several scriptural precedents which support the concept of providential protection and provision for God's people during times of divine judgment or adversity. For example, in the Old Testament Israel was divinely sheltered and protected during the successive outpourings of God's judgments upon the nation of Egypt. In spite of the fact that God's judgment severely crippled the nation of Egypt and brought her to her knees, Israel remained unscathed in the sheltered sanctuary of Goshen land. In this incident, God did not remove Israel from Egypt until after he had completely devastated the nation. The Israelites exited only after Egypt had been crushed under the repeated blows of God's wrath.

Besides this glaring precedent, there are several other minor examples. The miraculous feeding of Elijah the prophet by ravens (I Kings 17:2-6) during the judgment of the three year drought upon Ahab's kingdom is another example of the divine protection and provision of God on behalf of His people during times of judgment. The sheltering of Rahab while the battle of Jericho raged around her; the preservation of the three Hebrew children in Nebuchadnezzar's fiery furnace; and the safeguarding of Daniel in the lion's den are further examples of divine care during times of tribulation and testing.

Whether we are referring to protection in the midst of divine judgment, or simply protection in the midst of the tribulational characteristics of this age, God is more than capable of singling out His people from the unsaved and sheltering them in the very midst of adversity, without removing them from the planet earth. This can hold true even during the most intense periods of God's wrath. As MacPherson noted,

> Even if all tribulation wrath was exclusively divine wrath (which it isn't), God would have no more difficulty in distinguishing between the

72

bad guys and good guys than He had when He visited Egypt with plagues.[2]

Exempted from Tribulation?

As I have previously emphasized, it would be incomprehensible to picture God afflicting His own church with wrath and punishment. It would be contradictory to His very character and divine purpose to inflict these woes upon His own body. It is unmistakenly clear that God's people will not suffer the wrath of God in whatever form. However, when we speak of wrath or tribulation being inflicted upon the church, we must determine whether God's divine program has guaranteed us unconditional immunity from such sufferings.

It should be pointed out that the wrath of God is an entirely different matter than satanic wrath or the wrath of man. Just because God has promised to spare us from His wrath, He has not guaranteed us total exemption from the wrath of man, satanic persecution, or tribulation. Nowhere in the scriptures has God provided complete innoculation from the pressures of persecution, opposition, or tribulation.

Tribulation and persecution have been two of the common ingredients of the Christian experience in this world. Even a casual survey of church history substantiates the reality of this statement.

. . . tribulation is no stranger to God's people. In varying degrees, it has been the common denominator of all ages. In a variety of forms, it has been the plight of all believers. There is nothing in the statements of Christ or the apostles to support the belief that Christianity has been granted immunity from tribulations. Even a cursory glance of church history reveals that the gospel age has been marked by repetitious tribulations for Christians. When we consider the millions who were butchered by the Roman emperors, martyred by the Catholic Inquisitions, tortured, imprisoned and banished, we recognize in a far broader sense that the entire age has been one of incredible tribulation for God's people.[3]

The scriptures contain no special exemption clause for the last generation which favorably relieves them from the peculiar distresses associated with their moment in history. What grounds do we have

---

2. Dave MacPherson, *The Incredible Cover-Up,* p. 111.
3. William R. Kimball, *What the Bible Says About the Great Tribulation,* p. 113.

to presuppose that God will remove the last generation of believers from this world and exempt them from the tribulations characterizing their time frame when He has not done so previously? Certainly, the scriptures provide no solid base of support for this assumption. On this point Ladd commented:

> It would be contrary to the entire history of God's dealings with His people both in the Old and New Testament dispensations if God should in the consummation of the age reverse Himself to do something He has never previously done, namely, to protect His people from the hostility of an evil age . . . When we contemplate the history of martyrdom, why should we ask deliverance from what millions have already suffered?[4]

The Comments of Christ

In Christ's prophetic appraisal of the church age, He warned His disciples that they would experience inevitable persecution and affliction throughout the course of this age:

> Then shall they deliver you up to be afflicted, and shall kill you: and ye shall be hated of all nations for my name's sake (Matt. 24:9; see also Mark 13:9-13 and Luke 21:12-17).

The entire gospel era has proven the accuracy of Christ's prediction. He did not prophesy absolute protection from such pressures.

There isn't a single New Testament passage which proves that Christ has granted us exemption from tribulation. At the very threshold of this age, Jesus affirmed that the Christian life was not one of ease, but one of repetitious tribulation:

> These things I have spoken unto you, that in me ye might have peace. IN THE WORLD YE SHALL HAVE TRIBULATION: but be of good cheer; I have overcome the world (John 16:33).

In the verses that follow, Jesus prayed for His disciples: "I pray NOT THAT THOU SHOULDEST TAKE THEM OUT OF THE WORLD, but that thou shouldest keep them from the evil" (John 17:15). The "keeping" from evil to which Jesus refers has nothing to do with a rapture removal from the sphere of danger.

---

4. George E. Ladd, *The Blessed Hope,* pp. 127, 158.

In our Lord's prayer for His own we find a striking confirmation that keeping necessarily implies the presence of danger: "I am no more in the world; and yet they themselves are in the world . . . Keep them" (John 17:11, 12). Jesus contrasts His absence from this earthly scene with the presence of His disciples here. The keeping is required by their presence in the sphere of danger. The plain implication is that were they absent from the world with the Lord, the keeping would not be necessary.[5]

Some might object, however, that Jesus was only interceding for His immediate disciples of the first century, and that these prayer passages have nothing whatsoever to do with our present generation. However, He added: "Neither pray I for these alone, but for THEM ALSO WHICH SHALL BELIEVE on me through their word" (John 17:20). The clear implications of this prayer for us today is that we will be kept (Greek, "tereo"—preserve or protected) from the evil of this world even though we may experience the pressures of tribulation. These verses say nothing about removal from the world. Jesus did not pray, "In the world there shall be tribulation . . . but I pray that you will be taken out of the world."

The Comments of Paul

Paul also informed the church that ". . . we must through MUCH TRIBULATION enter into the kingdom of God" (Acts 14:22). Though he had strongly affirmed that we are not appointed unto God's wrath (I Thess. 1:10), he plainly stated that we are appointed to experience tribulation:

> That no man should be moved by these afflictions: for yourselves know that WE ARE APPOINTED THEREUNTO. For verily, when we were with you, we told you before that WE SHOULD SUFFER TRIBULATION, even as it came to pass, and ye know (I Thess. 3:3, 4).

As far as Paul was concerned, tribulation was the normal lot of the Christian experience. Paul saw a divine purpose in the tribulations we experience (II Cor. 4:16-18), and, for this reason, he could exhort us to glory in our tribulations and not in our escape from them (Rom. 5:3). God has not purposed that we should expect an exemption from

---

5. Robert H. Gundry, *The Church and the Tribulation*, p. 58.

the tribulations of this age, especially by placing wistful hopes on a secret rapture escape.

In a similar vein, Paul encouraged the Thessalonians in his second epistle to expect their ultimate deliverance from the tribulations inflicted upon them by the ungodly at the second coming of Christ:

> So that we ourselves glory in you in the churches of God for your patience and faith in all your persecutions and tribulations that ye endure: which is a manifest token of the righteous judgment of God, that ye may be counted worthy of the kingdom of God, for which ye also suffer: seeing it is a righteous thing with God to recompense tribulation to them that trouble you; and to you who are troubled rest with us, when the Lord Jesus shall be revealed from heaven with his mighty angels, in flaming fire taking vengeance on them that know not God, and that obey not the gospel of his power; when He shall come to be glorified in his saints, and to be admired in all them that believe (because our testimony among you was believed) in that day (II Thess. 1:4-10).

In this text, Paul assures the believers that they would be granted "rest" from their troubles "when (at the time) the Lord Jesus shall be revealed from heaven with his mighty angels, in flaming fire taking vengeance on them that know not God . . . when he shall come to be glorified in his saints."

These passages clearly reveal that Christians will weather the opposition and tribulations imposed by men until the second coming of Christ with His mighty angels. This coming "in flaming fire" to punish the wicked with "everlasting destruction" coincides with His coming "to be glorified in the saints." The scriptures do not say that He will return to deliver His people from tribulation and to be glorified in His saints secretly, seven years (or three and a half years) before He unleashes His final destruction upon our tormenters. However, until that blessed day arrives, we are to anticipate a continuance of tribulations.

The final round of tribulations, in whatever degree of intensity, whether they originate from the characteristic distresses of the times, the opposition of men, or the persecutions of an antichrist are nothing more than a culmination of the same hostilities which the world and the powers of darkness have generated against God's people since the fall of Adam.

Though God will not always physically deliver us from such tribulation (John 17:15), He will preserve us in them. Jesus assured us that even in death, not a hair of our heads would perish (Luke 21:16-18). Whether the tribulations of the days immediately preceding His coming are severe or mild, localized or wide-spread, physical or spiritual, God has promised to "never leave us or forsake us" (Heb. 13:5). Whether we must physically endure the troubles of the last days, or are called upon to face martyrdom, Christians have the positive guarantee that "to live is Christ, and to die is gain" (Phil. 1:21). We can take confidence in the fact that they may kill our bodies, but they cannot kill our souls.

The Rapture and Revelation — Chapters 4-19

Pretribulationists point to several other pertinent passages in defense of the position that the church will be absent from the earth during a final period of end-time chaos and wrath. They commonly claim that Revelation 4:1 marks the terminal point of the church's earthly sojourn with the rapture, and the beginning of the apocalypse which will supposedly follow:

> After this I looked, and behold, a door was opened in heaven: and the first voice which I heard was as it were of a trumpet talking with me; which said, Come up hither, and I will shew thee things which must be hereafter (Rev. 4:1).

This verse simply describes the revelation of things to come which John received in visionary form after he was called up to heaven. Pretribulationists, however, contend that John is actually a symbol of the church being raptured from the planet earth prior to the commencement of the awesome events portrayed in chapters 4-19. This belief is based upon the assumption that the phrase "come up hither" characterizes the rapture, and the word "hereafter" refers to the tribulational events which will transpire after the church has been removed from the earth.

However, a closer examination of Revelation 4:1 proves that it has nothing, whatsoever, to do with a pretrib rapture. First of all, the reference in this verse is not addressed to the church but to the Apostle John, and it was John who was in the Spirit and taken up into heaven. To equate John with the church is a purely arbitrary inference. As Woodrow noted:

77

John being thus taken up does not prove we should look for the church in heaven any more than his being taken in the spirit into the wilderness to "Babylon," would prove the church was there! (Rev. 17:3-5). Those who claim to "clearly" see a pre-tribulation rapture of the church in this verse must assume (among other things) that John is a type of the church. But John could not be a consistent type of the church in heaven during the period covered by chapters 4-18, for sometimes during those chapters he is represented as being back on EARTH! In Revelation 10:1 and also 18:1, for example, he sees an angel "come (not go) down from heaven"—wording which would place him below heaven in these scenes. In Revelation 11:1, in vision, he measures the "temple," which apparently does not symbolize something in heaven, for it is pictured as having a court which is given to the "Gentiles" to tread down. Then in Revelation 13:1, John is standing upon the sand of the sea, and a beast rising up out of the water appears, etc. John is sometimes pictured as being in heaven and sometimes on earth. He cannot, therefore, be a consistent representation of the church in heaven during these chapters.[6]

When commenting upon this verse, Neilson raised this additional objection:

First, Revelation 4 does not even say that John himself was lifted up from earth to heaven, let alone mention any future rapture of the church. John only says that he was in the spirit after the words spoken to him: "Come up here, and I will show you what must take place hereafter." It is only assumption that he was actually caught up to heaven, and not just seeing in a vision. Nowhere does it say he actually went up. Further, even if he were actually caught up, it is only assumption that his being caught up represents the rapture of the church. Moreover, additional interpretation has to be justified, namely, that all that occurs in chapter 4 and thereafter is yet totally future and does not apply to and is not being fulfilled in the present church age. . . . John was to write of things that would shortly take place, for the time was at hand. People were exhorted to heed the words of the prophecy —the whole inference being that what was seen would have a direct bearing in the concrete experiences of God's people, and was not just an encouragement built solely on blessing in some remote future.[7]

Furthermore, a careful examination of this verse reveals that the word "hereafter" (Greek: *meta tauta*) is the same identical term

---

6. Ralph Woodrow, *Great Prophecies of the Bible*, p. 34.
7. Lewis Neilson, *Waiting For His Coming*, p. 207.

employed at the beginning of this verse in the original. Revelation 4:1 both begins and ends with this phrase. But pretribulationists claim that the expression "hereafter" in the sentence, "Come up hither, and I will shew thee things which must be HEREAFTER" refers to the things which will happen after the church has been raptured. However, to endeavor to force this phrase to mean "after the church has been removed" in the second instance and not in the first is a flagrant example of exegetical inconsistency.

A careful review of the Greek phrase "meta tauta" reveals that it is a familiar expression in John's writings, though it is occasionally translated differently in our English version (John 3:22; 5:1; 5:14; 6:1; 7:1; 13:7; Revelation 1:19; 4:1 (twice); 7:1; 9:12; 15:5; 18:1; 19:1; 20:3). To arbitrarily enforce a meaning upon this expression in Revelation 4:1 when none of John's other usages of this term does so is an unwarranted breach of sound Biblical interpretation.

Pretribulationists contend that Revelation 4:1 marks the transition verse between the church's earthly position characterized by the seven churches of Asia (chapters 2-3), and its rapture to a heavenly position prior to the tribulation period. As Scofield stated:

> This call seems clearly to indicate the fulfillment of I Thessalonians 4:14-17 (the rapture). The word "church" does not again occur in the Revelation till all is fulfilled.[8]

Defenders of this belief frequently point to the marked absence of the church after verse 4:1. Walvoord's comments typify this familiar pretrib emphasis:

> It is notable that in this extended portion of Scripture not one mention of the church, the body of Christ, is found. . . . After the message to the seven churches in Asia . . . not one reference is found to the church, either by the name itself or by any other title peculiar to believers of this present age.[9]

Supporters of this position stress that since the church is repeatedly referred to in chapters 1-3, but is never specifically referred to in chapters 4-18, that it is only reasonable to assume that it is to be absent from the earth during this time. They claim that the church only

---

8. Cyrus I. Scofield, *Scofield Reference Bible,* p. 1334.
9. John F. Walvoord, *The Rapture Question,* p. 46.

re-emerges in chapter 19 during the Marriage Supper of the Lamb. But it is not mentioned directly until chapter 22, verse 16.

However, a closer look at the book of Revelation shows that this "assumption" is actually an unjustified "presumption." Pretribulationists fail to indicate that the church isn't specifically mentioned by name in chapters 19-21, either, where it is predominantly portrayed in symbolic form. Though the church is never mentioned in conjunction with any of the tribulation scenarios on earth, pretribulationists also conveniently ignore the fact that the church is not mentioned in any of the heavenly scenarios either. Furthermore, if we were to carry their line of reasoning through we would create a interpretive nightmare. As Gundry commented:

> The church is not mentioned as such in Mark, Luke, John, II Timothy, Titus, I Peter, II Peter, I John, II John, or Jude, and not until chapter 16 of Romans. Unless we are prepared to relegate large chunks of the New Testament to a limbo of irrelevance to the church, we cannot make the mention or omission of the term "church" a criterion for determining the applicability of a passage to saints of the present age.[10]

Though the church is not directly mentioned in chapters 4:1—22:15 of Revelation, an honest examination of this section demonstrates that the church is indeed referred to. The word "saints," which is an obvious reference to those who comprise the church, is mentioned several times (see Revelation 5:8; 8:3, 4; 11:18; 13:7, 10; 14:12; 16:6; 17:6; 18:24; and 19:8). For example, in Revelation 13:7 we read, "And it was given unto him to make war with the saints." Revelation 13:10 refers to the "patience and the faith of the saints" during their persecution. Revelation 16:6 speaks of the blood shed by the saints. Revelation 17:6 refers to the woman who was "drunken with the blood of the saints, and with the blood of the martyrs of Jesus." Revelation 18:24 also mentions the saints in conjunction with her atrocities against them: ". . . in her was found the blood of prophets, and of saints."

· Pretribulationists would readily admit that Revelation 1:5, 6 is a clear reference to the church:

> Unto him that loved us, and washed us from our sins in his own blood, and hath made us kings and priests unto God and his Father; to him be glory and dominion for ever and ever. Amen.

---

10. Robert H. Gundry, *The Church and the Tribulation*, p. 78.

However, there is an undeniable parallel between the thoughts contained in these verses and the reference in Revelation 5:8-10 which speaks of the "prayers of the saints" who were redeemed by the blood of Christ: ". . . out of every kindred, and tongue, and people, and nation; and hast made us unto our God kings and priests: and we shall reign on the earth." This promise to reign was specifically promised to the church (Rev. 2:26, 27).

While pretribulationists admit that the word "saint(s)" is mentioned in chapters 4-18, they usually brush aside the argument that it represents the church with such sweeping statements as:

> While there is frequent mention of "saints" both in heaven and on earth, that is obviously a general reference that could apply to believers in any dispensation.[11]

However, this argument represents nothing more than a begging of the issue.

Pretribulationists often dismiss this argument by claiming that the saints in question are not referring to the church, but to a specific group of tribulation saints often identified with natural Israel. This is a typical maneuver of pretribulationists when attempting to address this issue. According to dispensationalists, these saints are not a part of the saints who comprise the church. But when dealing with the use of the word saints in connection with the Marriage Supper of the Lamb (chapter 19), they do a flip-flop and claim it refers to the church in this instance. As Scofield affirmed, "The Lamb's wife here is the bride, the church."[12]

But the rules of proper interpretation dictate that if pretribulationists can argue that the saints in Revelation 19 refer to the church, then how can they reasonably argue that the saints mentioned in the previous chapters are not bonafide church saints? The reliability of such an erratic method of interpretation is highly questionable.

Revelation 3:10

Another supposed proof text of pretribulationists is Revelation 3:10. For example, Ironside flatly stated:

---

11. John F. Walvoord, *The Rapture Question,* p. 46.
12. Cyrus I. Scofield, *Scofield Reference Bible,* p. 1348.

The great tribulation cannot begin while the members of Christ's body are still upon the earth; for the Lord says to the church of this dispensation: "Because thou hast kept the word of my patience, I also will keep thee from the hour of temptation which shall come upon all the world to try them that dwell upon the earth" (Rev. 3:10).[13]

Walvoord also added, "A clear reference to the rapture is found in Revelation 3:10-11.[14]

However, posttribulationists are equally adamant in claiming that this verse offers little consolation for the pretribulational position. The pivotal issue of debate revolves around the Greek terminology in this verse. Pretrib supporters claim that the Greek term "terein ek" employed in this verse means to "keep from" rather than to "keep in," as posttribulationists maintain. Ryrie qualifies the dilemma as follows:

Posttribulationists say that "from" (ek) refers to protection of the church while within the Tribulation. Pretribulationists understand it to mean preservation by being absent from the time of tribulation. One is an internal protection (while living through the Tribulation); the other is an external protection (being in heaven during that time).[15]

Their line of reasoning follows that if the wording is indeed "keep from," then this "keeping from" must necessitate a removal in the form of a pretrib rapture. However, Gundry raised this perceptive question concerning the application of the phrase, ". . . keep thee from the hour of temptation":

The presence of danger is implicit in the idea of guarding. But if the church will be in heaven during the hour of testing, where will be the danger which would require God's protecting hand upon her?[16]

A thorough examination of this passage and its context reveals that the pretrib position is based upon pure conjecture.

The same Greek expression (terein ek) is also employed in John 17:15. This is the only other parallel scripture which uses this term:

---

13. H. A. Ironside, *Lectures on Daniel the Prophet*, p. 240.
14. John F. Walvoord, *The Rapture Question*, p. 255.
15. Charles C. Ryrie, *What You Should Know About the Rapture*, pp. 114, 115.
16. Robert H. Gundry, *The Church and the Tribulation*, p. 58.

I have manifested thy name unto the men which thou gavest me out of the world: thine they were, and thou gavest them me; and they have kept thy word. . . . I pray not that thou shouldest take them out of the world, but that thou shouldest keep them from the evil (John 17:6, 15).

The similarities between these verses and Revelation 3:10 are striking. Since both passages are recorded in the writings of John and each were spoken by Christ, a comparative study can shed light on the intended application of each verse. Though pretribulationists interpret "terein ek" to mean "to keep from," the usage of this term in John 17:15 clearly counters this interpretation. As LaRondelle commented:

This appeal to the meaning of the Greek is refuted, however, by Jesus' use of the same Greek verb in John 17:15, where he places this expression ("to keep from") in full contrast to the idea of removing the church out of the world. Instead, Christ promises protection that results in a victorious rescue through God's keeping power.[17]

LaRondelle further observed:

To say, as Walvoord does, that Christ's promise in Revelation 3:10 indicates a rapture of the church before the hour, or time, of tribulation is to shift Christ's emphasis away from the experience of the church during that time to the period of tribulation itself. But since a rationalistic distinction fails to catch the idiom in which an "hour" refers not to mere passage of time but to a prominent experience or trial (see John 2:4; 7:30; 8:20; 12:23, 27; 13:1).[18]

The people referred to in these verses have each kept the word, and because of this, God promises to keep them. In Revelation 3:10, they are kept from the "hour of temptation" (trial or tribulation); in John 17:15 they are kept from "the evil." In spite of the fact that one verse specifies that they are kept from the "hour of temptation" and the other states that they are kept from "the evil" it does not significantly alter the essential meaning, simply because evil and temptation are often close companions. Temptation (trials) are often designed to lead us into wrong-doing (see I Cor. 7:5; 3:5; Gal. 6:1; Matt. 26:41; Luke 4:13; 8:13; 11:4; I Tim. 6:9; and James 1:13, 14).

---

17. Hans K. LaRondelle, *The Israel of God in Prophecy,* p. 193.
18. Ibid., p. 193.

In the Lord's prayer, the disciples were instructed to pray ". . . lead us not into temptation, but deliver us from evil" (Matt. 6:13). It stands to reason that if we are kept from temptation, then we are consequently kept from evil. In both of these passages (Rev. 3:10 and John 17:15), believers are "kept from" evil or temptation. John 17:15 openly states that our keeping from evil would be accomplished without the bodily removal of the church from the sphere of evil's presence. If it is possible to be in the world and yet be kept or preserved from the evil influence of the world, then why is it not equally possible to be kept from the hour of temptation without being taken out of the earth?

The entire realm of temptation is not foreign to the Christian experience whether it is minor or acute, temporary or prolonged, isolated or widespread. Paul even revealed that temptation was a common dilemma of all men. However, Christians have been provided a special assurance:

> There hath no temptation taken you but such as is common to man: but God . . . will not suffer you to be tempted above that ye are able; but will with the temptation also make a way to escape, that ye may be able to bear it (I Cor. 10:13).

Our deliverance from temptation, in whatever form, is guaranteed because the Lord provides avenues of escape in our situations. However, this promised "escape" does not come in the form of a rapture out of our temptation. If this was so, the rapture experience would be a common experience in the life of most Christians. "The Lord knoweth how to deliver the godly out of temptations . . . ." (II Peter 2:9). What is more, He has been successfully accomplishing this for centuries without evacuating a single Christian from the planet earth! An examination of the key expressions used in the texts under consideration reveals that believers can "be kept from" the world's evil (John 17:15), can be "delivered out of temptations" (II Peter 2:9), and can be provided "a way of escape" (I Cor. 10:13) without being raptured from this present world.

Revelation 3:10 is not a subtle suggestion that God's promise to keep the Philadelphians equates to mean that they would be physically withdrawn from the midst of coming temptation. Instead, this verse simply stresses God's keeping power in the face of the "hour of temptation." This emphasis upon God's keeping power is also mentioned in several other companion verses. But none imply a rapture out of the world:

> But the Lord is faithful, who shall stablish you, and KEEP YOU FROM EVIL (II Thess. 3:3).

> Who are KEPT BY THE POWER OF GOD through faith unto salvation ready to be revealed in the last time (I Peter 1:5).

> Now unto him that is able to KEEP YOU from falling . . . (Jude 24).

The scriptures are filled with promises of God's preserving power in the midst of adversities (see Gen. 28:15; Ps. 31:23; 37:28; 57:1; 91:1-16; 121:5; Prov. 2:8; Isa. 25:4; John 17:11; II Tim. 1:12; and II Tim. 4:18).

Another problem concerning Revelation 3:10 involves its historic application. Though this verse mentions the hour of temptation "which shall come upon all the world, to try them that dwell upon the earth," pretribulationists run into difficulty in trying to force this verse into the straitjacket of a seven year (or 3-1/2 year) tribulation period. Even Walvoord, when commenting upon the issue of historic application, admits the limitation of this verse: "Its force and support of pretribulationism may be subject to qualification."[19]

Several pertinent points need to be considered in regards to the actual application of this prophecy to the history of the church as a whole. First of all, if this prophecy was specifically addressed to the Philadelphian church, contemporary with the Apostle John and located in Asia Minor, we must inquire whether this church was indeed kept from a world-wide time of temptation? If so, then how was it kept or preserved? Was it kept by means of a pretribulation rapture? If the actual application of this prophecy was intended for the first century Philadelphians, then they must have been kept by the power and grace of God rather than a rapture removal from the sphere of temptation since no evidence of a first century rapture is recorded in history.

Secondly, if these prophecies to the seven churches of Asia have a general application to Christians of all ages, then the promise of divine preservation is a comfort to every believer during their seasons of adversity and tribulation.

---

19. John F. Walvoord, *The Rapture Question*, p. 257.

Thirdly, if we accept the widely accepted perspective that the seven churches of Asia represent the seven successive periods in church history, then the pretribulational position is seriously weakened. If this verse is implying a rapture of the church before a distinct period of end-time tribulation, it should have been addressed to the seventh church (Laodicea) and not the sixth church (Philadelphia). Otherwise, you end up with a partial rapture of the majority of the church with a lukewarm remnant left behind. But the promise of being "kept from the hour of temptation" was not addressed to the seventh church. In other words, for Revelation 3:10 to accurately reflect the rapture of the church at the end of the age just before the Great Tribulation as pretribulationists claim, the chronological sequence of the seven churches would not be 1,2,3,4,5,6,7 but 1,2,3,4,5,7,6.

Luke 21:36

Luke 21:36 is also used by pretribulationists as a proof text for claiming a bodily deliverance of saints prior to an end-time tribulation period:

> Watch ye therefore, and pray always, that ye may be accounted worthy to escape all these things that shall come to pass, and to stand before the Son of man.

They interpret "all these things" to mean the terrors of a Great Tribulation, and the word "escape" to mean a rapture from that tribulation. Christ did admonish His disciples to "pray always, that (or to the end) ye may be accounted worthy to escape . . . ," but His statement is not a veiled promise of divine evacuation of believers to heaven before the commencement of a final tribulation.

We must determine what the word "escape" is in reference to. Escape from what? A closer look at the context reveals that the reference is intimately linked to "that day" mentioned in verse 34. It is quite apparent that "that day" refers to the time when God will suddenly unleash catastrophic destruction upon the earth at His return:

> And take heed to yourselves lest at any time your hearts be overcharged with surfeiting, and drunkenness, and the cares of this life, and so THAT DAY come upon you unawares. For as a snare shall it come on all them that dwell on the face of the whole earth. Watch ye therefore, and pray always, that ye may be accounted worthy to escape all these things that shall come to pass, and to stand before the Son of man (Luke 21:34-36).

The entire warning focuses upon the potential danger of being caught unawares at that day due to the stupifying characteristics of the times preceding the second coming. It is clear that that day can be nothing but the awesome and glorious coming of Christ. His sober caution is directed against the possibility of lapsing into a state of spiritual stupor, "lest THAT DAY come upon you unawares" (Greek: *aiphnidios* — suddenly, unexpectedly). On this point Woodrow perceptively noted, "Obviously, it could not come upon them unawares if they were to be raptured out seven years before the end of the age."[20]

The promise of escape from "all these things" has a twofold application:

> In Luke 21:36, we are admonished to watch and pray "that we may be accounted worthy to escape all these things . . . and to stand before the Son of man." We are cautioned to remain spiritually awake so that we may insure our escape from "these things"; however, the escape which Christ refers to is not a speculative pretribulation rapture prior to a supposed period of great tribulation. The immediate context reveals what these things are in reference to, and how we may safely escape them. The "these things" from which we may escape are both the debilitating influences of surfeiting, drunkenness, and the cares of this life, as well as the awesome terrors and wrath which will suddenly consume them who are overcharged with the prevailing influences of those days preceding Christ's return in judgment. Our sole guarantee for successfully weathering the potentially corruptive characteristics of that time will be through the steadfast maintenance of our spiritual vigilance. The coming of Christ will be as unexpected as the sudden springing of a fowler's snare upon "all them that dwell on the face of the whole earth" (Luke 21:35). But it will not be the deadly snare of sudden judgment for those who remain awake.[21]

Our sole guarantee for escape is intimately linked with our state of spiritual readiness and, for this reason, Christ repeatedly exhorts us to "WATCH YE THEREFORE, and PRAY ALWAYS, that ye may be accounted worthy to escape all these things" (Luke 21:36). As Thomas noted:

> . . . Christ is not telling us to pray that we may escape the great tribulation, but to pray for strength of soul to go through with it. We are

---

20. Ralph Woodrow, *Great Prophecies of the Bible,* p. 39.
21. William R. Kimball, *What the Bible Says About the Great Tribulation,* p. 232.

to pray for grace to escape the prevailing worldliness and pre-occupations which will engross mankind when Christ suddenly appears as the Judge of all.[22]

In other words, those who are devoted to Christ shall escape the surfeiting, drunkenness, and the cares of this life and, having accomplished this, will not fall prey to the final judgment which will suddenly overtake the world; or as Peter said, ". . . having escaped the corruption that is in the world through lust" (II Peter 1:4), we shall also escape that great day of destruction and wrath at the second coming of Christ. Nothing in this verse implies a secret rapture, and reading a rapture into this verse is totally unwarranted by the context.

Wrath in Revelation

Many believe that the book of Revelation indicates that prior to the final day of wrath there will be an extended period embodying the visitation of God's wrath upon a godless and corrupt humanity. Some maintain that this wrath will last for seven years; others believe it will last for only three and a half years; still others believe that God will reserve the outpouring of His wrath for a final, cataclysmic blast at the very end. It is not the intent of this book to dwell upon the truths contained in the book of Revelation concerning the exact nature, intensity, or duration of God's wrath, but one interesting fact concerning the focus of God's wrath should be clarified: It is never directed against the saints. This can be easily substantiated by examining the recipients of the last three "woes" and the seven "bowl" judgments. Furthermore, the Greek word for "wrath" (Greek: *thumos*), employed in Revelation, means a "violent outburst of fierce anger." It is used in nine out of its eighteen occurrences in the New Testament to represent divine wrath against the wicked. It is never directed towards the righteous (see Rev. 14:8, 10, 19; 15:1, 7; 16:1, 19; 18:3; 19:15). The Greek word *orge* is used five times in referring to God's wrath upon the ungodly (Rev. 6:16, 17; 14:10; 16:19; 19:15). These words are never used to apply God's wrath to His people.

---

22. Lawrence R. Thomas, *Does the Bible Teach Millennialism?* p. 82.

Comfort in Thessalonians

Another lesser used argument of pretribulationists centers upon the issue of whether I Thessalonians 4:13-18 offers genuine comfort to the church if, as posttribulationists contend, saints will first have to endure a tribulation period prior to the resurrection. Walvoord's comments are typical:

> . . . Posttribulationists have never satisfactorily explained why the Thessalonian Christians were not warned of the coming great tribulation when the hope of the rapture was extended to them as a comfort . . . though not totally ignoring this point, posttribulationists have still to explain how the Thessalonians could derive any comfort whatever out of a posttribulational rapture. . . . Generally, posttribulationists tend to ignore the problem of how a posttribulational rapture could be a comfort. . . . The prospect of the rapture after the tribulation is small comfort to those facing martyrdom. It is not too much to say that this is a most difficult problem to posttribulationists; as a group they tend to evade it rather than face up to it.[23]

In another work by the same author, he also raised a similar objection:

> . . . in I Thessalonians 4, the Thessalonians are told to be comforted and encouraged by the fact that the Rapture could take place at any time and that if so, they could be reunited with their loved ones who had died. To offer this as a comfort to them, if as a matter of fact, they had to survive the Tribulation in order to enjoy the Rapture and in the process face rather certain martyrdom, makes the exhortation of I Thessalonians 4:18 a hollow one indeed, if the posttribulationists are right.[24]

However, a closer examination of this argument proves that the prospects of comfort afforded by these verses are not minimized in the slightest. First of all, pretribulationists conveniently fail to indicate that the comfort of I Thessalonians 4:13-18 was written to believers who were already in the midst of intense persecution and tribulation. This is borne out by such passages as "having received the word in MUCH AFFLICTION, with joy of the Holy Ghost" (I Thess. 1:6); "for ye also have suffered like things of your own countrymen" (I Thess. 2:14); "that no man should be moved by these afflictions"

23. John F. Walvoord, *The Blessed Hope and the Tribulation*, pp. 152, 104, 105.
24. John F. Walvoord, *The Rapture Question*, p. 209.

(I Thess. 3:3); "we told you before that we should suffer tribulation; even as it comes to pass, and ye know" (I Thess. 3:4); and "so that we ourselves glory in you . . . for your patience and faith in ALL YOUR PERSECUTIONS AND TRIBULATIONS THAT YE ENDURE" (II Thess. 1:4). When viewed against the existing backdrop of the Thessalonian experience, we must ask whether Paul's exhortation to "comfort one another" loses any force because they were presently experiencing tribulation.

Secondly, pretribulationists presumptuously assume that this promise of comfort carries little weight if the church must weather intense tribulation, or even martyrdom, before the rapture occurs. They seem to suggest that the real significance of this passage rests fundamentally upon an exemption from a final period of tribulation. However, this assumption raises some serious questions. I must inquire whether this text has lent any less comfort to those Christians which have already passed through the terrors of tribulation? Regardless of the degree of severity during previous periods of tribulation, the undeniable fact is that millions of saints have already experienced the unimaginable terrors of tribulation resulting in martyrdom, torture, disfigurement, and imprisonment. Did Paul's consolation in Thessalonians have any less applicability for them? Was the comfort in this passage, or any other passage, nullified or minimized during their seasons of distress? An acceptance of this premise amounts to a total undermining of the timeless quality of Paul's comfort and, in effect, renders it meaningless as far as the majority of the church age is concerned. If we accept this premise, we end up isolating the aspect of comfort contained in these verses to those who will escape the Great Tribulation only. This would be a convenient argument for pretribulationists only if the church had not already victoriously weathered countless periods of intense tribulation.

Are pretribulationists on safe scriptural grounds in contending that the only realistic dimension of comfort can come by means of a pre-tribulation removal from the sphere of tribulation? If so, how do we reconcile this with such statements as:

> In the world ye shall have tribulation: BUT BE OF GOOD CHEER; I have overcome the world (John 16:33b).

> And not only so, BUT WE GLORY IN TRIBULATIONS ALSO (Rom. 5:3a).

For unto you it is given in the behalf of Christ, not only to believe on him, BUT ALSO TO SUFFER FOR HIS SAKE (Phil. 1:29).

My brethren, COUNT IT ALL JOY WHEN YE FALL INTO DIVERS TEMPTATIONS [trials] (James 1:2).

How can we ignore the dimension of hopefulness, purpose, and consolation indicated in these verses? Do we relegate them to meaninglessness along with hundreds of other comfort passages? To say that the only genuine comfort in I Thessalonians 4:13-18 is conditioned upon a pretrib rapture does not stand up to the acid test of scripture— quite the contrary. Apart from minimizing the Christian's genuine sense of comfort, experience has conclusively demonstrated that the promises and assurances of God's Word actually become more precious and promising in the very midst of adversity.

In closing, I would like to include the candid confession of another pretribulationist on this point:

Paul concludes his description of the rapture with comfort. Why? Does he offer comfort because the church will not go through the tribulation? No, he says nothing about the tribulation or the time of the rapture. It is comfort regarding the fact of the resurrection, not the *time* of the resurrection. "Be comforted in that your believing loved ones will live again." That is all Paul is saying. A post-trib, just as much as a pre-trib, can be comforted in that his loved ones will live again. Such comfort has nothing to do with the time of the rapture. Suppose for a minute that you had to go through the tribulation. You would still have the comforting thought that your believing loved ones will live again, wouldn't you? You see, even going through the tribulation does not wipe out this comfort that Paul is talking about. To derive a pre-trib implication from this comfort is as unrelated as grabbing for an apple in a bag of oranges.[25]

---

25. Allen Beechick, *The Pretribulation Rapture,* pp. 94, 95.

5

When Will Believers Be Separated from Unbelievers?

Advocates of a pretribulation rapture teach that believers will be separated from unbelievers seven years prior to the second coming of Christ in judgment. Many stress that this world-wide event will happen unexpectantly, silently, and will be shrouded in secrecy. We will now tackle this issue in an attempt to determine when this decisive cleavage between believers and unbelievers will take place.

The Wheat and the Tares

Posttribulationists often refer to the companion parables of "the tares and the wheat" and "the dragnet" (Matt. 13) as passages which pinpoint the precise timing of separation. As Neilson noted,

> The parables . . . buttress the impression of one final coming of Jesus Christ at the end of the age, with that coming and end bringing a termination of opportunity of salvation and a separation of the righteous and the wicked.[1]

---

1. Lewis Neilson, *Waiting For His Coming,* p. 99.

And Gundry added: "The gathering of the wheat (verse 30) and of the good fish (verse 48) then represent the rapture, which is thereby posttribulational."[2]

Christ clearly specified that the righteous would not be separated from the wicked until the end of this age. He presented this fact in parabolic form (Matt. 13:24-30). In the parable of "the wheat and the tares," He compared the kingdom of heaven to "a man which sowed good seed in his field" and "while men slept, his enemy came and sowed tares among the wheat and went his way" (Matt. 13:24b, 25). When the crop had come to fruition, the servants discovered what had happened:

> So the servants of the householder came and said . . . wilt thou then that we go and gather them up? But he said, Nay; lest while ye gather up the tares, ye root up also the wheat with them. Let both grow together until the harvest: and in the time of harvest I will say to the reapers, Gather ye together first the tares, and bind them in bundles to burn them: but gather the wheat into my barn (Matt. 13:27-30).

Jesus did not leave us in the dark to speculate about the intended meaning of this parable. He provided the interpretation:

> He that soweth the good seed is the Son of man; the field is the world; the good seed are the children of the kingdom; but the tares are the children of the wicked one; the enemy that soweth them is the devil; the harvest is the end of the world; and the reapers are angels, and they shall gather out of his kingdom all things that offend, and them which do iniquity, and shall cast them into a furnace of fire: there shall be wailing and gnashing of teeth (Matt. 13:37-42).

This parable indicates that the time of separation of the tares from the wheat will be at the "END OF THE WORLD." Jesus stressed that both would grow together until the end of the world, and then the harvest would occur, thus resulting in a simultaneous separation between the wheat and the tares.

However, in order for pretribulationists to remain consistent, the wheat and the tares would not grow together until the end of the world, for they presuppose that the wheat crop will have to be harvested sooner. In essence, the wheat would have to be garnered before the end of the age. This very point is defended by Scofield: "At the end of this age the tares are set apart for burning, but first the wheat

2. Robert H. Gundry, *The Church and the Tribulation*, p. 142.

94

is gathered into the barn.''[3] This is a blatant reversal of the order presented in this parable. Christ emphasized that the tares were to be gathered first for burning, and then the wheat was to be gathered into the barn. If both the wheat and tares are said to remain together in the field until the harvest at the end of the world, then the idea of the church (wheat), or any portion thereof, being removed (raptured) from the earth seven years prior to the tares is a contradiction of the scriptural order presented in this parable.

Alexander Reese addressed the issue of order as follows:

> But if anything was lacking to refute Darbyists' explanation of the parable, it is found in their treatment of the burning of the tares. The wording of the parable, "Gather ye together *first* the tares, and bind them in bundles to burn them: but gather the wheat into my barn" (verse 30), and the words of the Lord's interpretation (verses 41-43), that the professors are gathered for judgment at the same crisis as the transfiguration of the righteous, naturally causes great embarrassment to men who separated them by several years.[4]

Pretribulationists attempt to circumvent the obvious lesson of this parable by claiming that this parable has nothing whatsoever to do with a pretrib rapture. For example, Walvoord flatly stated that,

> In a word, Matthew 13 does not discuss the doctrine of the rapture at all, and there is absolutely nothing in this passage that would contradict the pretribulational view.[5]

Though they readily admit that Christ is establishing the timing of separation, they restrict the application of this parable to the second coming and not to a pretribulation rapture. Matthew 13 says nothing about a pretrib rapture, and pretribulationists seize upon this fact by arguing from a position of silence that it has supposedly occurred earlier. This is a clever way of evading the pretrib problem.

Beechick addresses this issue at length, and speaks in behalf of of many pretribulationists on this point. While he agrees that the scenario depicted in this parable is indeed posttribulational, he argues that the pretrib rapture is not even in question. As far as he is concerned, it doesn't even enter the picture. He takes it for granted that the rapture would have already transpired prior to the fulfillment of the harvest of wheat and tares. Since the order presented in this

---

3. C. I. Scofield, *Scofield Reference Bible*, p. 1016.
4. Alexander Reese, *The Approaching Advent of Christ*, p. 98.
5. John F. Walvoord, *The Blessed Hope and the Tribulation*, p. 85.

parable seems to contradict the order presented elsewhere (Christ coming to earth first for the righteous followed by judgment upon the wicked), pretribulationists presuppose that the rapture must have transpired earlier:

> A rapture seven years earlier, seven years before the time of harvest, does not enter into the order of gathering at all. Suppose I told you to buy eggs on Monday. Then on Friday, told you to buy meat and eggs in that order—meat first, eggs second. Would you conclude that you were not supposed to buy eggs on Monday because the order would be wrong? Of course not! The order on Friday has nothing to do whatsoever with the purchase on Monday. Likewise, the order of harvest at the end of the tribulation has nothing to do with the rapture at the beginning of the tribulation. A pre-tribulation rapture does not interfere in any way with the order of gatherings in the time of harvest. The rapture does not keep saints and sinners from growing together until the end of the age. The rapture does not interfere with the main point of the parable, that the wicked are not to be rooted out until the end. The rapture does not interfere with a gathering of the righteous after the wicked. At no point does a "pre-trib" rapture make this parable untrue.[6]

Though this pretribulational argument might seem convincing on the surface, it contains some serious weaknesses. One of the principal issues raised in this parable is that the tares are not to be rooted out lest we run the risk of uprooting the wheat in the process. For this reason, Christ restricted the harvest to the end of the world. But logic necessitates that the reverse is also true. If there was a pre-rooting out of the wheat seven years before the harvest, then the tares would be conversely rooted out also. This would violate the parable as well. Christ stressed, "LET BOTH GROW TOGETHER UNTIL THE HARVEST" (Matt. 13:30a). His command undermines any notion of a pre-uprooting of either wheat or tares until the end.

This verse says nothing of a pre-harvest of wheat seven years before the final harvest at the end of the world. But pretribulationists are presuming a previous harvest of wheat in the form of a pretribulation rapture. However, there isn't the slightest suggestion of a pretribulation harvest of wheat prior to the great harvest, which is the focal point of this parable. If we accept the pretribulational position, the

---

6. Allen Beechick, *The Pretribulation Rapture,* p. 197.

wheat in question amounts to nothing more than an isolated stand of wheat left over to be gleaned at the end after the primary harvest of wheat has already been accomplished seven years earlier. However, in reality, if the wheat were harvested, there wouldn't be any left over at the final gathering. As Boettner put it, "If the dispensational theory were true, namely, that the church is raptured out of the world, there would be left only the tares."[7]

This argument is built upon the sands of pure conjecture and pre-supposition—certainly not upon scriptural fact. Pretribulationists are in gross violation of context, and are guilty of attempting to force the clear thrust of this parable into the strict framework of pre-tribulational teaching. Their aribitrary inferences are hopelessly misleading and amount to little more than a blatant case of "eisegesis" (a reading into a text what is not there).

Though pretribulationists delight in raising an objection against the order of gathering presented in this parable in relationship to a post-tribulational perspective, the difficulty is not insurmountable. As Gundry noted:

> It is objected against the interpretation that in the parable the wicked are gathered before the saints whereas at the Parousia the saints will be gathered prior to the judgment of the wicked. But the objection is not entirely convincing. Although the tares are bound or prepared for burning before the gathering of the wheat, the actual burning, or judgment, is not stated to occur before the gathering of the wheat and may, instead, occur afterward in the field.[8]

Concerning this objection, Boatman also added:

> Actually, which is taken first is an academic question. It will all happen too closely together to make any real difference. This is true also of the resurrection of the righteous dead and the rapture of the righteous saints. In either case, while the one precedes the other, yet it all takes place the same day (Luke 17:28-30), even the same hour (John 5:28, 29), yea, even "in a moment, in the twinkling of an eye" (I Cor. 15:51, 52).[9]

In the companion parable of "the dragnet," the timing of separation between believers and unbelievers is also pinpointed. Jesus further

---

7. Lorraine Boettner, *The Millennium*, p. 170.
8. Robert H. Gundry, *The Church and the Tribulation*, pp. 142-143.
9. Russell Boatman, *What the Bible Says About the End Time*, p. 199.

likened the kingdom to a net which was cast into the sea. When it was drawn to shore, it contained both good and bad fish. The good were placed into vessels, but the bad were cast away.

Jesus provided the interpretation of when this separation would transpire:

> So shall it be at the END OF THE WORLD: the angels shall come forth, and sever the wicked from among the just, and shall cast them into the furnace of fire (Matt. 13:49-50a).

In both of these parallel parables, the precise timing of separation is specified. However, Walvoord argues that the parable reverses the order presented in the parable of "the wheat and the tares": ". . . the opposite order is given in connection with the good and bad fish that are separated in Matthew 13:48, with the good fish selected first."[10] But Beechick, another pretribulationalist, disagrees. He claims that, "In the companion parable of the fishnet, the angels 'sever the wicked from among (literally, out of the mist of) the just' (Matt. 13:49). The order is repeated."[11] Walvoord has apparently overlooked verses 49-50. The process of gathering the good fish into the vessels takes place after the selected segregation of the bad fish. As Christ indicated,

> So shall it be at the end of the world: the angels shall come forth, and SEVER THE WICKED FROM AMONG THE JUST, AND SHALL CAST THEM INTO THE FURNACE OF FIRE (Matt. 13:49-50a).

Both parables clearly indicate a process of sorting and separation between the righteous and the unrighteous in conjunction with His return. There is nothing recorded to suggest a severing of the righteous prior to the wicked—especially in terms of years.

Furthermore, it is important to note that Jesus specified the exact timing of separation in both of these parables. This is important for the simple reason that doctrine must be constructed upon the clear statements of scripture rather than upon symbolic or parabolic expressions which are subject to a wide range of speculative opinions. Based upon the clear wording of Jesus, the end of the world will mark the time when those who belong to Him will be spared, while destruction will be the portion afforded the wicked.

---

10. John F. Walvoord, *The Rapture Question,* p. 184.
11. Allen Beechick, *The Pretribulation Rapture,* p. 195.

"As It Was in the Days of Lot"

Jesus further likened the timing of separation of believers from unbelievers to the day when Lot exited the city of Sodom:

> . . . as it was in the days of Lot; they did eat, they drank, they bought, they sold, they planted, they builded: But the SAME DAY that Lot went out of Sodom, it rained fire and brimstone from heaven, and destroyed them all. EVEN THUS SHALL IT BE IN THE DAY WHEN THE SON OF MAN IS REVEALED (Luke 17:28-30).

According to the clarity of Christ's statement, believers will be removed from of the outpouring of God's wrath on the "SAME DAY" that fiery destruction will fall upon an unregenerate humanity, even as righteous Lot was delivered on the same day in which the unbelievers of Sodom and Gomorrah were annihilated. The passage does not say that Lot was removed from Sodom seven years before the judgment consumed the cities of the plain. It specifically states that the separation was a simultaneous event transpiring on the "SAME DAY."

As if to reinforce the reality of this truth, Jesus also compared His second coming to the judgment of the flood upon Noah's generation:

> And as it was in the days of Noe [Noah], so shall it be also in the days of the Son of man. They did eat, they drank, they married wives, they were given in marriage, UNTIL THE DAY THAT NOE ENTERED INTO THE ARK, AND THE FLOOD CAME, AND DESTROYED THEM ALL (Luke 17:26, 27; see also Matt. 24:37-41).

Jesus plainly indicates the timing of separation between believers and unbelievers. Noah was spared and the unbelieving remnant was simultaneously destroyed. The destruction produced a great separation. So shall it be at the Second Coming of Christ.

In both comparisons, Jesus stresses the timing of separation. Both isolate the timing to the "same day." As Wilmot noted:

> The simultaneous action of God in deliverance and judgment our Lord drew attention to when He spoke of His coming, and like incidents in Biblical history, are not wanting. "The day (the selfsame day: Gen. 7:11-13) that Noah entered the ark, the flood came and destroyed them all"; "the same day that Lot went out of Sodom, it rained fire and brimstone from heaven and destroyed them all." "Even thus shall it be when the Son of man is revealed" (Luke 17).[12]

---

12. John Wilmot, *Inspired Principles of Prophetic Interpretation*, p. 195.

In commenting upon the wording in these passages, Carver added this perceptive challenge:

> What did our Lord believe as to the character of His return? Was it to be a two-phased event? . . . Our Lord indicates that the days preceding His return will witness a world identical in character with the world before the Flood, and the cities of the plain before the great catastrophe engulfed them. Verses 27, 28, and 29 describe the exact nature of His coming; note carefully our Lord's words:
>
> UNTIL THE DAY THAT NOAH ENTERED INTO THE ARK, and the flood came and DESTROYED THEM ALL.
>
> The same day that Lot went out of Sodom it rained fire and brimstone from heaven and DESTROYED THEM ALL.
>
> EVEN THUS SHALL IT BE in the Day when the Son of Man is revealed.
>
> If, in the light of these statements of our Lord, men can still talk about a two-phased coming . . . then words have ceased to have any intelligible meaning. To say our Lord held these ideas is totally inconceivable in the face of this language . . . there was no confusion with our Lord. It is His constant testimony; and it is the unbroken witness of every New Testament voice. As the judgment of the flood sealed the irretrievable doom of all the ungodly, whilst the righteous were secure; and as the Lord delivered just Lot on the day that the fire engulfed the ungodly, SO IT WILL BE AGAIN. In the great Day of His Revelation, His redeemed people will be gathered to eternal safety and peace, whilst the ungodly shall perish in the fearful judgment that shall wrap the world in flames.[13]

Many pretribulationists openly acknowledge that the scenarios depicted in the companion illustrations of Noah and Lot represent a posttribulational setting. They agree that the timing of separation presented in these texts is clearly at the second coming. For example, in defending this posttribulational context, Beechick admits: "Luke 17 provides further powerful proof of the order of gatherings."[14] However, as with the parables of "the wheat and the tares" and "the dragnet," they seek to minimize the impact in timing by claiming that these verses have nothing to do with a pretribulation rapture. This is a convenient scheme of pretribulationists when dealing with those passages which spell irretrievable shipwreck to their position.

---

13. Arthur Carver, *The Great Consummation*, p. 30.
14. Allen Beechick, *The Pretribulation Rapture*, p. 204.

They clearly circumvent the issue by claiming that the rapture is not even in question in these passages. They simply presuppose a prior pretribulation rapture before the events characterized by Noah and Lot even transpire.

However, this manuever is nothing more than exegetical gymnastics. With this sort of exegesis, an interpreter can add to or delete anything he wants from the scriptures. This interpretive tactic is only a desperate attempt to accommodate a pretribulation rapture outside the framework of these second advent passages. Pretribulationists recognize that these verses lend strong support to the opposing school, so they are forced to defend their position on purely presuppositional grounds. They must resort to this tactic or be compelled to accept the reality that the separation of believers from unbelievers coincides with the timing of Christ's second coming.

In Conjunction with Judgment

Though the antedeluvian world of Noah's day was destroyed by water, the Apostle Peter informs us that the present world will be destroyed by fire:

> Whereby the world that then was, being overflowed with water, perished: But the heavens and the earth, which are now, by the same word are kept in store, reserved unto fire . . . (II Peter 3:6, 7).

He further describes the manner in which the existing world will be destroyed by fire:

> But the day of the Lord will come as a thief in the night; in the which the heavens shall pass away with a great noise, and the elements shall melt with fervent heat, the earth also and the works that are therein shall be burned up (II Peter 3:10).

One thing seems to stand out in Peter's characterization. He stresses that the coming of the Lord "as a thief" shall be accompanied with devastating fury at the climax of this age.

In the immediate context of these statements, he cautions believers:

> Seeing then that all these things shall be dissolved, what manner of persons ought ye to be in all holy conversation and godliness. LOOKING FOR AND HASTING UNTO THE COMING OF GOD, wherein the heavens being on fire shall be dissolved, and the elements shall melt with fervent heat? (II Peter 3:11, 12).

The wording of Peter's text clearly specifies that the day which will witness the worldwide conflagration of unbelieving humanity is the same day that believers are exhorted to be "looking for and hasting unto." However, if believers are to be removed from the earth seven years before this cataclysmic end, then why would Peter bother to warn believers to be "looking for and hasting unto the coming day of God, wherein, the heavens being on fire shall be dissolved, and the elements shall melt with fervent heat?" (II Peter 3:12). "Surely he would not attempt to encourage them by something that will happen at the end of the age, if their real hope was an event to take place seven years earlier."[15]

Peter reveals that "the day of the Lord will come as a thief in the night" (verse 10). Peter links this characterization to the time when "the heavens shall pass away with a great noise, and the elements shall melt with fervent heat." His statements closely parallel the comments of Paul which intimately link "the day of the Lord" which "cometh as a thief in the night" to the catching up of the saints:

> For the Lord himself shall descend from heaven with a shout . . . Then we which are alive and remain shall be caught up. . . . in the clouds, to meet the Lord in the air: and so shall we ever be with the Lord. Wherefore comfort one another with these words. But of the times and the seasons, brethren, ye have no need that I write unto you. For yourselves know perfectly that the day of the Lord so cometh as a thief in the night. For when they shall say, Peace and safety; then sudden destruction cometh upon them, as travail upon a woman with child; and they shall not escape (I Thess. 4:16—5:3).

When commenting upon this section, Boettner stated:

> . . . in I Thessalonians 5:1-4, which follows immediately after the passage from which Dispensationists think to derive their doctrine of a secret Rapture (4:16, 17), Paul's words make it clear that he is not talking about a seven year Rapture at all, but rather the day of the Lord or Judgment Day. . . . This passage [I Thess. 5:3, 4) shows that instead of the righteous being taken away before the Judgment Day, they are here right up until the time the wicked receive their punishment. . . .[16]

---

15. Ralph Woodrow, *Great Prophecies of the Bible,* p. 14.
16. Lorraine Boettner, *The Millennium,* p. 167.

102

William Grier added:

Paul associates the second coming with the resurrection and the ensuing glory of saints and the sudden destruction of the wicked. Without the shadow of doubt, that day has its reference to both parties:—believers are to look for it (I Thess. 5:4-10), for then they shall obtain salvation in all its fulness (verse 9), then they shall "live together with him" (verse 10); while that same day will bring the false security of unbelievers to an end in their "sudden destruction."[17]

Concerning the obvious inter-relationship of II Peter 3 and I Thessalonians 5, Neilson included this observation:

Chapter 5 of I Thessalonians is quite interesting in view of our discussion of II Peter 3. Paul, after discussion of the rapture in chapter 4, then reiterates that the disciples need nothing written about "the times or seasons," only a reminder that the day of the Lord will come like a thief in the night, catching the wicked unprepared as contrasted with believers, coming suddenly and bringing destruction so that the wicked do not escape. II Peter 3 spoke of the day of the Lord, and destruction of ungodly men. Also, this day of the Lord was termed day of God, both being a day of fire and transformation to the new heavens and earth.[18]

A careful correlation of these companion texts demonstrates that the "day of the Lord" which "cometh as a thief in the night" is the time when Christ will descend from heaven with a shout, believers will be resurrected and caught up to rendezvous with the Lord in the air, sudden destruction will fall upon an unbelieving world in fiery form, and the present heavens and earth shall pass away with a great noise.

"In Flaming Fire"

Another key text which indicates the timing of separation is found in II Thessalonians:

And to you who are troubled rest with us, when the Lord Jesus shall be revealed from heaven with his mighty angels, in flaming fire taking vengeance on them that know not God, and that obey not the gospel

---

17. William J. Grier, *The Momentous Event*, p. 71.
18. Lewis Neilson, *Waiting for His Coming*, p. 73.

of our Lord Jesus Christ: who shall be punished with everlasting destruction from the presence of the Lord, and from the glory of his power; when he shall come to be glorified in his saints . . . . (II Thess. 1:7-10a).

The saints are said to receive their ultimate relief from their sufferings and tribulation at the same time that God recompenses the ungodly with judgment. Nothing indicates a previous deliverance from the pressures of this age seven years prior to the time of divine retribution upon the wicked.

> We may notice that when the Savior comes for the deliverance of His troubled saints, He comes "in flaming fire"—no secret rapture here! But it is even more important still to notice how the reward of the righteous and the punishment of the wicked are interwoven with each other as to time, and made to follow, both of them, immediately on the coming of the Lord.[19]

These verses, then, clearly reveal that the scheduled relief for the righteous coincides with divine judgment upon the wicked at the second coming of Christ. Wilmot's comments are worthy of consideration at this point:

> The descent of the Lord from heaven, then, will be with a view to joyful release and retributive judgment; release for the righteous and retribution for the wicked will be executed in the event of His one coming. "When he shall come to be glorified in his saints" is said to be the same time "when the Lord Jesus shall be revealed from heaven in flaming fire taking vengeance," without separating stages and interval of years. He will then release His church from all the persecutions and tribulations she has endured. . . . At this time He will in righteous judgment visit vengeance upon their foes. The simultaneity is enforced by the repeated "when," and "in that day" reinforces the timing so that the human arrangement of a two-stage coming is rendered altogether untenable (II Thess. 1).[20]

"The Last Day"

The scriptures clearly teach that the catching up of the saints coincides with the resurrection. Therefore, the precise timing of the

---

19. William J. Grier, *The Momentous Event,* pp. 71, 72.
20. John Wilmot, *Inspired Principles of Prophetic Interpretation,* p. 194.

resurrection is important. The scriptures reveal that the resurrection of the saints will transpire on the last day. For example, in the aftermath of Lazarus' death, Martha confronted the Lord and acknowledged that her brother would "rise again in the resurrection AT THE LAST DAY" (John 11:24).

It is important to note that Martha's resurrection perspective was not based upon empty Jewish tradition or vain speculation, for Christ repeatedly confirmed this truth as well:

> And this is the Father's will which hath sent me, that of ALL which he hath given me I should lose nothing, but should RAISE IT UP AGAIN AT THE LAST DAY (John 6:39).

> And this is the will of him that sent me, that EVERYONE which seeth the Son, and believeth on him, may have everlasting life: AND I WILL RAISE HIM UP AT THE LAST DAY (John 6:40).

> No man can come to me, except the Father which hath sent me draw him: AND I WILL RAISE HIM UP AT THE LAST DAY (John 6:44).

> Whoso eateth my flesh, and drinketh my blood, hath eternal life; AND I WILL RAISE HIM UP AT THE LAST DAY (John 6:54).

Certain obvious conclusions can be drawn from these statements. Since the catching up of the saints is synonymous with the resurrection of the dead in Christ (I Thess. 4:16, 17), it is plain to see that the rapture will take place "AT THE LAST DAY," and not seven years prior to the last day. Furthermore, the language in these verses leaves little room for uncertainty. Jesus used the words "all" and "everyone" when referring to those believers who would be resurrected, and also specified that it would happen on the "last day." Certainly He didn't imply "all" with some exceptions, "everyone" minus a pretrib company, or "last day" give or take seven years. "All" doesn't leave much room for omissions. Neither does "last day" leave room for last day plus seven years!

Pretribulationists seek to downplay the forcefulness of the phrase "last day" by stretching the term to include the entire period from the commencement of a final tribulation period until the end. They are forced to adopt this tactic in order to facilitate a pretribulation rapture. However, the actual application of the phrase "last day" (not last days) is self-explanatory. It leaves little room for the pretribulationist theory of an extended time frame. The adjective "last" is quite explicit, in spite of the fact that some pretribulationists try to relegate it to relativity.[21] The overwhelming burden of proof rests upon pretribulationists in attempting to prove that the term "last day" doesn't mean exactly what it says. In reality, the pretribulationist argument amounts to defining the word "last" as "almost last," or "last" with measurable qualifications.

"The Last Trumpet"

The scriptures not only associate the resurrection with the last day, but also tie it to the sounding of the "last trumpet." In the two key rapture passages we read:

> For the Lord himself shall descend from heaven with a shout, with the voice of the archangel, and with the TRUMPET of God: and the dead in Christ shall rise first: then we which are alive and remain shall be caught up together with them in the clouds, to meet the Lord in the air (I Thess. 4:16, 17, NKJV).

> Behold, I tell you a mystery: we shall not all sleep, but we shall all be changed—in a moment, in the twinkling of an eye, at the LAST TRUMPET. For the trumpet will sound, and the dead will be raised incorruptible, and we shall be changed (I Cor. 15:51, 52, NKJV).

The similar information in these events is significant. Each mentions the sounding of "the trumpet," even though in the later passages the trumpet is called "the last trumpet." Both refer to the resurrection of the dead saints, and each alludes to the transformation which will occur when believers are caught up to meet the Lord.

In commenting upon the timing of the resurrection and rapture indicated in these texts, Neilson stated:

> . . . I Corinthians speaks only of a resurrection of Christ the first fruits, and then those at his coming. No mention is made of multiple resurrections or multiple changes in connection with his coming. It is at the last trumpet that the dead are raised. This reminds us of the trumpet that accompanies the resurrection in I Thessalonians 4. At the last trumpet, the last enemy is destroyed. Further resurrections or changes of God's people are precluded.[22]

---

21. Allen Beechick, *The Pretribulation Rapture*, p. 95.
22. Lewis Neilson, *Waiting for His Coming*, p. 96.

With these trumpet passages in mind, we compare another corresponding scripture:

> And I saw the seven angels which stood before God; and to them were given seven trumpets (Rev. 8:2).

As each trumpet sounds in the series, certain events take place. But what transpires with the sounding of the seventh trumpet, the last in the series, is strikingly similar to the two trumpet passages we have previously examined:

> And the seventh angel sounded; and there were great voices in heaven, saying, The kingdoms of this world are become the kingdoms of our Lord, and of his Christ; and he shall reign for ever and ever. And the nations were angry, and thy wrath is come, and the time of the dead, that they should be judged, and that thou shouldest give reward unto thy servants the prophets, and to the saints, and them that fear thy name, small and great; and shouldest destroy them which destroy the earth (Rev. 11:15, 18).

The obvious relationship of these passages is significant. Each includes the same essential ingredients: 1) The trumpet sounds—the seventh and last; 2) The time of the dead to be raised—the resurrection; and, 3) The saints are rewarded, which would include their being transformed from corruptible to incorruptible, from mortal to immortality, and being caught up to meet the Lord in the air.

The scriptures we have reviewed strongly suggest that the rapture will be at the end of the age, at the last day, at the last trumpet. But according to pretribulational interpretation, the rapture would have to take place at the time of the first trumpet or before, simply because the church will be gone when the trumpets of Revelation are sounded. But Revelation 11:18 clearly states that the sounding of the seventh trumpet is in conjunction with the time of wrath upon the nations, the time for the dead to be judged, and the time to "give reward unto thy servants the prophets, and to the saints, and them that fear thy name, small and great . . . ." In light of these glaring truths, we find it difficult to accept the teaching that the saints will be raptured before any of the trumpets are sounded. The timing of the rapture is restricted to the seventh, or last trumpet.

107

Though pretribulationists deny the relationship of these verses on the supposed ground that the trumpets mentioned by Paul are entirely different trumpets from the ones referred to in Revelation 8-11, their arguments are based more upon conjecture than scriptural fact. Wilmot included this interesting observation concerning the relationship of Paul and John's trumpet passages:

In the liberty and prescience of the Holy Spirit, however, Paul was inspired thus to designate the trump, and John later to write the explanation. Moreover, John, by command of the Lord Jesus, both Paul's Lord and John's, addressed the first of seven letters in this Apocalypse to Ephesus, to whom Paul had earlier written. It was said that at the beginning of the sounding of the seventh trumpet, "the mystery of God" would be completed "as he had declared to his servants the prophets." That doubtless has a Pauline and Ephesian flavour! The mystery concerns the preaching of the unsearchable riches of Christ, and thereby, the building of the church, elect and saved of Jews and Gentiles, the one body, one new mankind, "the fulness of him that filleth all in all," a completeness indeed. Time for this will be no longer, but thereupon the time of resurrection and judgment and reward and wrath will have arrived. The completion of the one means the institution of the other. The time when the mystery of God will be finished, therefore, will not be reached until the events announced under John's seventh trumpet. And John's seventh is the last, agreeing both in title, time and substance with Paul's "last trumpet." Of this same time John wrote: "And the nations were angry and Thy wrath is come; and the time of the dead that they should be judged; and that Thou shouldest give reward unto Thy servants the prophets, and to the saints, and them that fear Thy name, small and great; and shouldest destroy them that corrupt the earth" (Rev. 10:5-7; 11:15-18). At this one and selfsame time, therefore, and not in intervalled stages, the Lord Jesus will finish the building of His church. . . . He will raise the dead unto judgment and reward His saints of all generations—the terms are as descriptively comprehensive as could be in such short space. He will then also, in the same event, at the same time, visit His wrath upon the wicked world.[23]

No Man Knows the Time

In conclusion, I would like to comment on Matthew 24:36 in relationship to the issue of timing in separation between believers

---

23. John Wilmot, *Inspired Principles of Prophetic Interpretation,* pp. 192-193.

and unbelievers. This verse stresses that no man knows the day or the hour of the end of the age.

> Regardless of the bold and persistent endeavors of datesetters to pinpoint the precise, or even approximate, timing of the Lord's return, His own words clearly establish the utter impossibility of such attempts, for even Jesus emphasized that it was unknown to Himself (Mark 13:32). If it was unknown to even the "incarnate word of God," then no mere mortal, no matter how prophetically enlightened he may be, will be able to clearly compute the timing of the second coming from his own calculations, natural observations, or from information contained within the Word.[24]

These verses stand as a formidable defense against pretribulationism for the very reason that if the rapture was to occur seven years before the last day, then multitudes of people would be able to calculate the exact date of His return. All they would have to do is to count seven years from the day when millions of people mysteriously disappeared from the planet earth. This possibility, however, would be in clear violation of Christ's comments to the contrary.

---

24. William R. Kimball, *What the Bible Says About the Great Tribulation,* p. 213.

6

Will Christ's Return
Be in Two Stages?

Though evangelical and orthodox Christians agree in a future, bodily return of Christ, controversy continues to surround the issue of whether there are distinct time phases or intervals associated with Christ's eventual return. Pretribulationists contend that the second coming will actually be divided into two distinct phases. For example, when addressing this issue LaHaye stated:

> The Second Coming of Jesus Christ is mentioned 318 times in the New Testament alone, but a careful examination of the passages reveals what appears at first to be conflicting concepts. For example, one passage tells us that Christ will come "in the air" (I Thess. 4:17), whereas another tells us he is coming "to the earth." One passage tells us that his coming is to be secret, "as a thief"; another tells us "every eye shall see him." One passage teaches that his coming will be a time of joy and blessing; another tells us the people of earth "shall mourn" . . . .
> The only way to correlate these teachings regarding Christ's coming is to understand that his coming is in two stages. The first stage is the Rapture, or taking away, of the church; the second is the Glorious

Appearing to the whole earth. Christ will come secretly in the Rapture; he will come to the earth at the Glorious Appearing. The Lord's coming will be a time of great joy when he raptures the church, but his coming to the earth will be a time of great sorrow for then he will destroy the wicked nations.[1]

They see the second coming splintered into two specific stages which are separated by either seven or three and a half years. Though they emphasize that they embrace only one second coming of Christ, their pretribulational stance necessitates a fragmentation of the second coming into two very distinct comings.

However, their arguments create some serious problems and inconsistencies. If, as pretribulationists claim, the rapture is a separate stage from the return of Christ in power and glory, then how could each stage be called the second coming? If the rapture and Christ's return in glory are two unique events, it would be impossible for each to be labeled the second coming. Simple logic dictates that these two events strongly suggest a second and a third coming of Christ.

At the timing of Christ's ascension to His Father, His bewildered followers stood watching. While they were viewing His ascension, two angels appeared and inquired:

Ye men of Galilee, why stand ye gazing up into heaven? This same Jesus which is taken up from you into heaven, shall so come IN LIKE MANNER as ye have seen him go into heaven (Acts 1:11).

It is quite apparent that the disciples did not witness Christ ascending to heaven in two separate phases, separated by a lengthy interval of time. They were specifically told that His return would be "in like manner," that is, a unified event. As Neilson noted, "The text certainly teaches a coming again of Christ from heaven, but there is nothing to indicate more than one coming. Based on the words alone one would expect only one coming again."[2]

Hebrews 9:26-28 also argues forcefully against a multi-staged second coming:

For then must he often have suffered since the foundation of the world: but now once in the end of the world hath he appeared to put away

---

1. Tim LaHaye, *The Beginning of the End*, p. 21.
2. Lewis Neilson, *Waiting For His Coming*, p. 55.

sin by the sacrifice of himself. And as it is appointed unto men once to die, but after this the judgment: so Christ was once offered to bear the sins of many; and unto them that look for him shall he appear the SECOND TIME without sin unto salvation.

This passage clearly reveals that the true hope which we look for is the second coming of Christ. In spite of this blatant reality, pretribulationists still attempt to defend a plurality of phases. As Wilmot pointed out, " 'He shall appear the second time' is the word of inspiration, but not a third. The contradiction occasioned by the futuristic theory is, therefore, overcome by the subterfuge of introducing the idea of one Second Coming in two stages."[3]

But as opponents of pretribulationism maintain, the wording in this passage is quite explicit. As Neilson noted:

> . . . Christ came once before to do all necessary by one sacrifice to put away sin. The whole crux of this portion is finality. At the end of the ages Christ came once to put away sin by his one sacrifice. . . . Just as Christ accomplished all appointed to him at his first coming, so he will come a second time (not a third, or fourth, etc.) to bring the final complete deliverance for all those who eagerly wait for him.[4]

When commenting upon this issue, LaRondelle also added:

> The vocabulary of the New Testament does not allow for the idea of two comings, or two phases of Christ's coming, separated by a seven year period of tribulation. It substantiates only one appearance of Christ in glory. . . . Inspiration states He will appear "a second time" (Heb. 9:28), not "two more times."[5]

Those who advocate that Christ will come for His church in one stage and then return seven years later in the second stage are actually teaching a doctrine not only of a second coming, but a third coming of Christ as well. But the idea of a third coming is totally foreign to biblical teaching. Such terminology is unheard of also. Those who maintain that there will be two parts of the second coming do so through their own assumptions and not the clear teaching of scripture. The Bible never refers to the second coming(s) plural, but of the Lord's

---

3. John Wilmot, *Inspired Principles of Prophetic Interpretation,* pp. 186-187.
4. Lewis Neilson, *Waiting For His Coming,* p. 80.
5. Hans K. LaRondelle, *The Israel of God in Prophecy,* p. 189.

second coming, singular. The very concept of two second comings is itself a ridiculous contradiction in terms. When weighed in the balance of scripture, the concept of a multi-staged second coming is found wanting.

Some dispensationalists ignore the problem altogether; while others labor to circumvent the inherent difficulty arising from their concept of two comings by arguing that the rapture is not really the coming of the Lord at all. For example, one author commented:

> Strictly speaking the rapture is not the second coming at all. The second coming is the visible, local, bodily appearing of Christ in the clouds of heaven as he returns to this earth . . . in power and great glory.[6]

Another wrote:

> The thrilling event which will both mark the end of the day of grace and open the door for the Great Tribulation is the rapture. . . . Specifically speaking, this is not the second coming of Christ. Rather this is the rapture, or the catching up, of the true church.[7]

Still another bluntly declared that the rapture is not the second coming and that, "The scriptures referring to the rapture could not refer to the second coming."[8] These are only a selection of the many dispensational writers who maintain that the rapture is not the second coming. However, their defense amounts to nothing more than a clever, exegetical maneuver.

Pretribulationists also attempt to evade the difficulties associated with a plurality of second comings by trying to stretch the term "second coming" to include both phases. For example, Bloomfield's comments are representative of many:

> The coming of Christ may be thought of as applying to the whole process, beginning with the Rapture and continuing till He comes in person to establish His kingdom.[9]

However, in spite of these and similar appeals, the Word of God provides a battery of scriptures pointing to only one second coming as the real hope of Christians. Nowhere is the pretribulationist idea of a

---

6. Frank M. Boyd, *Ages and Dispensations*, p. 60.
7. William W. Orr, *Armegeddon and the End of the World*, p. 99.
8. J. G. Hall, *Prophecy Marches On!*, Vol. 2, pp. 36, 39.
9. Arthur E. Bloomfield, *Signs of His Coming*, p. 15.

plurality of returns stated or implied. The revelation of New Testament chronology concerning the Lord's advent makes allowance for only one consummate coming of Christ. The scriptural testimony does not support a multiplicity of second comings. As Neilson again affirmed, "Nowhere in Matthew – Jude is it stated that there are two future comings."[10] With these affirmations, the New Testament witness is in unanimous agreement.

In Matthew 24:44, Jesus warned the church, "Therefore be ye also ready: for in such an hour as ye think not the Son of man cometh." This and parallel statements were repeatedly given by Christ (see Matt. 24:42, 50; 25:13; Mark 13:33; Luke 12:40). In the face of such repeated cautions, I must ask why Jesus would take such pains to warn us about being ready for the Son of man if, in reality, what we are really to be ready for is a secret rapture seven years before His coming?

In Revelation 16:15 we read: "Behold, I come as a thief. Blessed is he that watcheth." This verse is clearly posttribulational in its context. So we must inquire why such a warning would be given about His coming if seven years before His coming believers would have mysteriously been raptured to heaven?

In commencing the parable of the pounds recorded in Luke, Jesus says:

> . . . A certain nobleman went into a far country to receive for himself a kingdom, and to return. And he called his ten servants and delivered them ten pounds, and said unto them, OCCUPY TILL I COME (Luke 19:12, 13).

The contents of this parable are clearly within a second coming context. This verse cautions believers to continue occupying (Greek: *pragmateomai* — to trade or do business) until He returns. But how can the church continue occupying until He comes if the church will "shut down shop" seven years before He returns?

In the gospel of John, Jesus provided the church with this timeless assurance:

> In my Father's house are many mansions: if it were not so, I would have told you. I go to prepare a place for you. And if I go and prepare a place for you, I will come again, and receive you unto myself; that where I am, there ye may be also (John 14:2, 3).

---

10. Lewis Neilson, *Waiting For His Coming,* p. 155.

Pretribulationists often cite this verse as a pretrib rapture proof text. While most posttribulationists admit that this verse is referring to the rapture, they do not see it in a pretribulational context. Christ said that He was preparing a place for us in reference to the many mansions or abiding places in the Father's house. The statement carries a distinct air of finality and consummation. This characterizes an abiding inheritance. But according to pretribulationists, this verse necessitates the church being raptured to their heavenly abode only to vacate it seven years later when they return to earth. According to their perspective, our heavenly mansion is either a mobile home or a temporary residency with a seven year lease.

Pretribulationists, like Walvoord, scoff at this argument by claiming that "heaven is something more than a place: it is where Christ is. The church will be with Christ wherever He is. . . ."[11] Though this perspective is true, it ignores the heart of Christ's promise which not only assures believers "that where I am, there ye may be also," but also makes a point of Christ's "preparing a place" for us in connection with the "many mansions" which are in His "Father's house." This verse not only refers to our intimate abiding with Christ, but promises us a permanent abiding place as well. But the pretribulational argument amounts to characterizing this abiding place as a temporary abode at best.

The Apostle Paul speaks of Christians as "waiting for the COMING of our Lord Jesus Christ" (I Cor. 1:7). But why would he mention our "waiting for" His "coming" if He really believed that Christians would be secretly raptured seven years before His coming? Why would Paul mislead believers by telling them to wait for an event which would happen seven years after they had already been raptured?

Paul prayed that the Thessalonians would be "preserved blameless unto the COMING of our Lord Jesus Christ" (I Thess. 5:23). But again, why would he pray for us to be preserved blameless unto the coming of Christ if the rapture is an event that will take place seven years before the Lord's coming?

In Hebrews we read:

> For ye have need of patience that, after ye have done the will of God, ye might receive the promise. For yet a little while, and he that shall COME will COME, and will not tarry (Heb. 10:36, 37).

11. John F. Walvoord, *The Blessed Hope and the Tribulation*, p. 91.

This passage clearly cautions believers to remain patient until the coming of Christ. But why focus upon the coming of Christ if our real hope rests upon an event slated to occur seven years before His coming?

In the same vein, James exhorted us to "Be patient then, brethren, unto the COMING of the Lord" (James 5:7). But why would James admonish believers to be patient unto the coming of the Lord if we are to be secretly raptured seven years before His coming?

Peter also challenged us to be,

> Looking for and hasting unto the COMING of the day of God, wherein the heavens being on fire shall be dissolved, and the elements shall melt with fervent heat (II Peter 3:12).

Why would Peter have specifically designated the coming day of God in which the heavens will be on fire and the elements will melt with fervent heat as the day Christians are to be "looking for and hasting unto" if what we are really "looking for and hasting (Greek: *speudō* — earnestly desire) unto" is a secret rapture seven years prior?

A general survey of these passages points out the obvious fact that the scriptures equate the coming of the Lord with the rapture. As far as Christ, Paul, Peter, and James were concerned, they were the selfsame event. The various expressions "occupy till I come," "waiting for the coming," "preserved blameless unto the coming," "patient . . . unto the coming," and "looking for and hasting unto the coming" all substantiate the reality that when the Lord comes, believers will be gathered up to meet Him.

This fact is particularly reinforced through the emphasis of Hebrews 9:28 which provides irrefutable proof that Christ will return only one "second time" for those who look for Him. This verse leaves no room for the notion of "second time," parts A and B. Though pretribulationists, with one fell swoop, ignore this glaring fact by characterizing all of the above passages as pertaining to a pretrib context, the bottom line of this defense amounts to stating that the second coming of Christ is really not what we are waiting for. But as convenient as this argument may be, it faces an insurmountable objection in the light of Hebrews 9:28. The preponderance of evidence is overwhelming that the rapture is not a separate stage or phase from the coming of Christ. This "second," second coming concept is simply a perversion of scriptural teaching.

7

Coming "For" and Coming "With" the Saints

Another area of controversy which commonly confronts both pre and posttribulationists centers upon the phraseology which refers to the Lord's coming "for" His saints and coming "with" His saints. Both parties have waged a running battle over this issue for years.

A Natural Assumption

In keeping with the two-stage theory of pretribulationism, the secret rapture will involve Christ's coming "for His saints" to be followed seven years later by His public appearance "with His saints." The phrases "for His saints" and "with His saints" are frequently employed to sustain the two-stage coming theory. The question is often raised, "How can Christ possibly come back 'with' His saints unless He has previously come 'for' His saints?" Pretribulationists hold this perspective as axiomatic. A widely circulated series of prophecy lessons stated the issue as follows:

We need to ever keep in mind that there will be a "second coming" and a "third coming" of Christ, which some writers prefer to speak of as the first and second phase of Christ's return. He will return "FOR His saints," and He will also return "WITH His saints": When He returns FOR His saints, then it is that He comes only in the clouds. But when He returns WITH His saints, then it is that His feet will once again stand on the Mt. of Olives.[1]

Blackstone summarized this pretribulational assumption as follows:

The Rapture occurs when the church is caught up to meet Christ in the air, before the tribulation; and the Revelation occurs when Christ comes, with His saints, to end the Tribulation, by the execution of righteous judgment upon the earth. At the Rapture, Christ comes into the air for His saints. At the Revelation, He comes to the earth with them. He certainly must come for them before He can come with them.[2]

On the surface, this argument seems quite persuasive; however, a thorough examination reveals that it contains a deceptively simplistic and superficial logic at best.

Proof Texts?

Only three passages include this distinctive phrase (Zech. 14:5; I Thess. 3:13; and Jude 14). But only the latter two are generally heralded by pretribulationists as supposed proof texts to bolster their concept of a coming "for" and a separate coming "with":

To the end he may stablish your hearts unblameable in holiness before God, even our Father, at the coming of our Lord Jesus Christ WITH ALL HIS SAINTS (I Thess. 3:13).

And Enoch also, the seventh from Adam, prophesied of these, saying, Behold, the Lord cometh WITH ten thousands of HIS SAINTS . . . . (Jude 14).

Each of these verses are definitive in describing the Lord's coming "with His saints." However, a closer examination of these verses reveals some serious weaknesses in the pretribulationist contention that the Lord's coming "for His saints" and "with His saints" are two distinct stages of Christ's return and are separated by a lengthy

---

1. Cited from *Thinking Through Thessalonians,* Wilbur Fields, p. 247.
2. William E. Blackstone, *Jesus Is Coming,* pp. 75-76.

interval of time. Fletcher challenges this pretribulation assumption as follows:

> This theory is a perversion of Second Coming truth, a delusion of the last days, widely held. Nowhere does the New Testament teach two future comings of Christ, first FOR His saints, and then WITH His saints some three-and-a-half to seven years later. Those who hold this view seek to harmonize it with the New Testament teaching on the Second Coming of Christ by asserting that the coming FOR and WITH the saints several years later are not two comings, but two stages of the Second Coming of Christ. This attempt to justify the theory cannot overthrow the testimony of the senses that the coming FOR the saints is a FIRST second coming, and the subsequent coming WITH the saints is a SECOND second coming. But this cannot be. He came once, and He will come once more—and only once more: "the second time without sin unto salvation" (Heb. 9:28).[3]

First of all, I should qualify the usage of the terms "coming for" and "coming with." Though the concept of the Lord's coming "for" His saints is verified by scriptural fact (John 14:3; I Cor. 15:23, 51; I Thess. 4:15-17; II Thess. 2:1), the expression "for the saints" is never employed. None of these passages couples the concept of the Lord's coming "for the saints" with the scriptural phrase "coming with the saints." As Fields affirmed:

> We observe first of all that the Scripture in NO place makes any distinction between Christ's coming FOR His saints, and His coming WITH His saints. It does not even use the expression, "coming FOR His saints." We would be the first to acknowledge that Christ is coming to take up His saints to be with Him, but to make a distinction between that coming and the coming WITH His saints is to make a distinction where the Scriptures make none.[4]

Who Are the "Saints"?

A careful consideration of the word "saints" referred to in these verses sheds invaluable light on the subject. The word saints is translated from the Greek word *hagios* and simply means "holy or holy one(s)."

3. George B. Fletcher, *Will a Secret Rapture Precede the Second Coming of Christ?* p. 2.
4. Wilbur Fields, *Thinking Through Thessalonians*, p. 248.

It is a common word in the New Testament and is found in over 240 references. The term is predominantly translated holy or holy ones. However, there is nothing inherent in the word itself to indicate who these holy ones are. Depending upon the context, the word *hagios* can either refer to angels or men. For example, the word is found in Deuteronomy 33:2; Daniel 4:13, 17, 23; 8:13; Matthew 25:31; Mark 8:38; Luke 9:26; Acts 10:22; and Revelation 14:10 where the obvious reference is to angelic beings. On the other hand, such passages as Deuteronomy 33:3, Daniel 7:18, 22, and Psalm 16:3 have an obvious reference to men. The overwhelming usage of the term *hagios,* whether translated "saint(s)" or a variation of "holy" or "holy one(s)," is unquestionably referring to men. But the supposed pretribulation proof texts under study (I Thess. 3:13 and Jude 14) face some strong objections when trying to force the term *hagios* (translated "saints") to apply to men who were previously raptured to heaven.

Literally translated, both passages refer to Christ's coming "with all His HOLY ONES" (I Thess. 3:13), and "with ten thousands of His HOLY ONES" (Jude 14). A careful comparison of the parallel statements of scripture characterizing the second coming with these two verses reveals the precise contextual application of the term "saints." Opponents of pretribulationism commonly maintain that the word *hagios* used in these passages is not speaking of men, but of the angelic accompaniment at Christ's return. Even one of the editors of the Scofield Reference Bible voiced his opinion that the *hagios* in I Thessalonians 3:13 was referring to angels and not men: "These saints or holy ones are the angels who in other scriptures are said to come with the Lord; they accompany him when he comes for the church as in this verse."[5] In commenting upon the application of the word *hagios* in Jude 14, one commentator noted, "The 'ten thousands of his saints' is better rendered 'ten thousands of his holy ones' . . . for the 'holy ones' here intended are the angels."[6]

Numerous passages correlate Christ's coming with angels. And, as I have previously indicated, they are occasionally referred to as holy angels (*hagios*). Jesus clearly taught that He would return with an angelic retinue. The gospels repeatedly clarify this fact:

---

5. William J. Eerdman, cited from *The Blessed Hope,* by George Ladd, p. 90.
6. Spence and Excell, *Pulpit Commentary, Vol. 22,* p. 12.

The Son of man shall send forth his ANGELS, and they shall gather out of his kingdom all things that offend, and them which do iniquity (Matt. 13:41).

So shall it be at the end of the world: the ANGELS shall come forth, and sever the wicked from among the just (Matt. 13:49).

For the Son of man shall come in the glory of his Father WITH HIS ANGELS; and then he shall reward every man according to his works (Matt. 16:27).

And he shall send his ANGELS with a great sound of a trumpet, and they shall gather together his elect from the four winds, from one end of heaven to the other (Matt. 24:31).

When the Son of man shall come in his glory, and all the HOLY ANGELS WITH HIM, then shall he sit upon the throne of his glory (Matt. 25:31).

Whosoever therefore shall be ashamed of me and of my words in this adulterous and sinful generation; of him also shall the Son of man be ashamed, when he cometh in the glory of his Father WITH THE HOLY ANGELS (Mark 8:38; see also Luke 9:26).

And then shall he send his ANGELS, and shall gather together his elect from the four winds, from the uttermost part of the earth to the uttermost part of heaven (Mark 13:27).

And to you who are troubled rest with us, when the Lord Jesus shall be revealed from heaven WITH HIS MIGHTY ANGELS (II Thess. 1:7).

That Christ will indeed return with the holy angels is an established fact. But whether His return will be coupled with a saintly entourage is still open to question. The real issue still boils down to whether Christ's coming with the saints, whether they be angels or men, will be preceded by His coming for the redeemed several years prior. By carefully examining I Thessalonians 3:13, we discover that this verse does not support the two-stage concept of a "coming for" and a "coming with," separated by a three-and-a-half to seven year interval.

"With All His Saints"

First of all, it is highly questionable that this verse could conceivably be referring to a coming of Christ "with ALL his saints" (I Thess. 3:13) simply because Paul was specifically praying that we (saints) might be established "unblameable in holiness before God . . . AT THE COMING of our Lord." No one could reasonably contend that the saints who had been previously raptured (resurrected and translated in body), and taken to heaven to be with Jesus three and a half to seven years earlier would need to be further established "unblameable in holiness" at His coming. As Fields so clearly noted,

Now surely no one could say that saints who had been resurrected and transformed in body, and taken up to be with Jesus would need to be further established unblameable in holiness. Only if they were here on earth would they need to be established in holiness when the Lord comes with all His people. They would have to be on earth where they needed to be established unblameable in holiness. And they would have to be with the Lord coming down from heaven at the same time, if the idea is true that the Lord is coming with all his people.[7]

In support of this view, Woodrow added:

In all probability, the meaning intended in this passage is simply that Paul desired the Thessalonians to be established in the faith and be found unblameable at the Second Coming—along with all the other saints—those at Corinth, Colossae, Ephesus, and all believers everywhere.[8]

In view of the foregoing information, it is highly unlikely that Paul's mention of Christ coming "with the saints" in this verse lends any support to the pretribulationist notion of a separate coming for the saints in the form of a secret rapture.

The assigned mission of the angelic host in connection with Christ's coming indicates that saints will be on the earth. The scriptures clearly teach that the angels will "sever the wicked from . . . the just" (Matt. 13:49), and they will "gather together his elect" from the entire earth (Matt. 24:31). The fact that saints will be on the earth proves that the phrase "with ALL His saints" has definite limitations. He can't possibly come with all the redeemed from heaven if millions will still be upon the earth when He comes.

If the phrase "with all His saints" characterizes Christ's coming with both men and angels, it still provides no support for the concept of two stages of Christ's coming. This verse, while not supporting the two-stage theory, does leave room for the inclusion of men and angels:

---

7. Wilbur Fields, *Thinking Through Thessalonians,* p. 248.
8. Ralph Woodrow, *Great Prophecies of the Bible,* p. 30.

The words "all his saints" are so comprehensive that it is difficult . . . to avoid the conclusion that both holy angels and men are referred to—all the holy ones of heaven. The only exception which the language of the passage seems to justify us in making concerns the living believers who will be on earth at the time of the coming.[9]

Those Who Sleep in Jesus

This interpretation fits nicely with the information given in I Thessalonians 4:14:

> For if we believe that Jesus died and rose again, even so them also which sleep in Jesus will God BRING WITH HIM.

This statement reveals that the dead in Christ will be brought with Him at His return. This verse is located in the immediate context of the principal rapture passage of I Thessalonians 4:13-18. The "bringing" of those who sleep in Jesus with Him at His coming is a simultaneous event with the rapture, the resurrection, and the translation of the living saints. It will not occur seven years after the rapture. The obvious conclusion is that when Christ returns at the time of the rapture with His holy angels, those who are dead in Christ will be brought with Him. As Allis so clearly indicated,

> When we compare this passage with iv. 14 . . . the natural meaning seems to be that when the Lord comes from heaven He will be accompanied by the angels and by the disembodied spirits (souls) of all the holy dead. While He is in the air . . . the bodies of the holy dead will be raised and these dead will be clothed upon with their resurrected and glorified bodies. Then the living, we that are alive that are left, will be "gathered together" (Matt. 24:31), will be "changed" (I Cor. 15:52), and "caught up" to meet the Lord in the air, and to come with Him and all His saints to the earth (Acts 1:11) . . . it will be both a coming for and a coming with: a coming with the saints already in heaven for the redemption of their bodies, a coming for the saints then on earth who are to be changed and caught up; and this coming with and for the saints into the air will be followed by a coming with the saints to the earth.[10]

---

9. Oswald T. Allis, *Prophecy and the Church*, pp. 186, 187.
10. Ibid., p. 187.

On this point, Carver also added this perceptive observation:

It will be well to point out first of all that the Coming of the Lord so graphically described in these verses (I Thess. 4:13-18, MINE) is said by futurists to be the Coming FOR His saints, as distinct from His Coming WITH His saints some years later. But in chapter 3, verse 13, Paul prays that these Thessalonians may be established unto "the Coming of our Lord Jesus Christ WITH all His saints." Now, not even a dispensationalist would attempt the fantastic claim that 3:13 represents a different Coming from 4:15. Then what becomes of this alleged distinction between the Coming FOR and Coming WITH? Like most other matters in this theory, it has existed only in the minds of the theorists. He will come "with" the dead in Christ, and "for" the living saints.[11]

Furthermore, I Thessalonians 3:13 cannot be used as a proof text for the notion of a coming "for" the saints as contrasted to a coming "with" the saints at a later date on the grounds of the New Testament usage of the word "coming" used in this verse. The word translated "coming" in this verse is taken from the Greek word "parousia." This is the very word which pretribulationists apply to the secret, first phase coming of Christ "for the saints" seven years before His open, glorious appearance "with His saints." But this verse describes His "coming ("parousia") with all his saints." Instead of teaching two stages of Christ's return, it simply reveals that the "parousia" is not the secret coming "for the saints," but the open coming of Christ to the earth. We will examine the issue of terminology associated with the second coming more extensively in the next chapter.

Jude 14

Jude 14 is also used by pretribulationists to defend the two-stage concept.

And Enoch also, the seventh from Adam, prophesied of these, saying, Behold, the Lord cometh WITH ten thousands of his saints.

The inference is again stated that if the Lord is coming "with" His saints, He must first of all have come "for" His saints. Pretribulationist

---

11. Arthur Carver, *The Great Consummation,* p. 72.

arguments concerning this passage parallel the same arguments used in I Thessalonians 3:13. However, the same rebuttal also applies. This verse, along with I Thessalonians 3:13, clearly refers to the Lord's coming "with" His saints. And though the word "saints" could include both men and angels in this great company, this verse lends absolutely no support to the concept of a prior coming "for" all the saints seven years earlier. Like its companion counterpart in I Thessalonians, the word "saints" is derived from the Greek word *hagios* and simply means "holy," or in this verse "holy ones." The expression "ten thousands of his saints" is literally translated "ten thousands of His HOLY ONES." As we have previously indicated, Jesus stressed that He would come again with His holy angels:

> When the Son of man shall come in his glory, and all the holy [*hagios*] angels with him (Matt. 25:31).

> Whosoever therefore shall be ashamed of me . . . of him also shall the Son of man be ashamed, when he cometh . . . with the holy [*hagios*] angels (Mark 8:38; Luke 9:26).

The phrase "ten thousands of saints" is also located in an Old Testament passage which is viewed as a clear reference to angels:

> . . . The Lord came from Sinai, and rose up from Seir unto them; he shined forth from mount Paran, and he came with TEN THOUSANDS OF SAINTS: from his right hand went a fiery law for them (Deut. 33:2).

The fact that angels are being characterized is substantiated by two related passages:

> The chariots of God are twenty thousand, even thousands of angels: the Lord is among them, as in Sinai, in the holy place (Ps. 68:17).

> Who have received the law by the disposition of angels, and have not kept it (Acts 7:53; see also Gal. 3:19).

Both passages link angels to the giving of the law at Mount Sinai. This harmonizes perfectly with the information contained in Deuteronomy 33:2. As Matthew Henry commented:

> His retinue was glorious; he came with his holy myriads, as Enoch had long since foretold he should come in the last day to judge the world, Jude 14. These were the angels . . . . They attended the divine majesty,

127

and were employed as his ministers in the solemnities of the day. Hence the law is said to be given by the disposition of angels.[12]

The parallel wording employed in this verse and Jude 14 cannot be easily dismissed. A comparison strongly suggests that the saints in question are referring to the angelic host who will return with Christ to execute vengeance and wrath upon the ungodly (Jude 15). We have repeatedly seen that angelic beings will participate in the final holocaust at the end of the age (Matt. 13:40-42; II Thess. 1:7). Jude 14, 15 is in complete harmony with this perspective.

Though there is room for men to be included in this company, there is no evidence that they would have been raptured from the earth seven years before this coming. As in the case of I Thessalonians 3:13, they would be the souls of those who were dead in Christ. As Matthew Henry noted, "The Lord cometh with his holy myriads, including both angels and the spirits of just men made perfect."[13] As Paul wrote, ". . . even so them also which sleep in Jesus will God bring with him" (I Thess. 4:14b).

"To Meet the Lord"

Another forceful argument against the two-stage theory focuses upon the meaning and application of the word "meet" employed in the key rapture text of Thessalonians:

> Then we which are alive and remain shall be caught up together with them in the clouds, to MEET the Lord in the air: and so shall we ever be with the Lord (I Thess. 4:17).

Pretribulationists claim that since the saints will be caught up to "meet" the Lord in the air that this heavenward ascent lends support to their defense of a two-stage coming. They naturally assume that our translation skyward is a clear indication of our heavenward destination immediately following our rendezvous in the air.

However, opponents of the two-stage concept argue just the opposite. They maintain that Christ's descent to the earth will be uninterrupted at the rapture. They claim that the scriptures say nothing about a

---

12. Matthew Henry, *Matthew Henry's Commentary, Vol. 1.*
13. Matthew Henry, *Matthew Henry's Commentary, Vol. 6, Jude.*

change of direction in the Lord's descent after the saints have joined Him in the air. Though pretribulationists like Walvoord maintain that, "First Thessalonians 4 says nothing about continuing the journey to the earth,"[14] it should be pointed out that this verse says nothing about a return trip to heaven either. On the basis of direct statements, neither posttribulationists or pretribulationists can conclusively prove their position. However, the internal evidence associated with the distinctive usage of the word "meet" lends strong support to the argument against the two-stage theory.

Interpreting this "meeting" of the Lord in the air by both the resurrected, dead saints and the translated, living saints to mean that Christ will then book them on His return flight to heaven to wait seven years before coming back to earth again violates the precise meaning of the word "meet." The word translated "meet" is derived from the Greek word *apantēsis*. It is a unique word used in reference to the coming of a king or magistrate to visit a city. As Bruce noted:

> When a dignitary paid an official visit or parousia to a city in Hellenistic times, the action of the leading citizens in going out to meet him and escorting him on the final stage of his journey was called the apantēsis. . . .[15]

A careful correlation of the manner in which this distinctive term is employed in other New Testament passages demonstrates that it contains essentially the same meaning. When King Jesus descends, believers will rise to meet Him in the clouds and then promptly proceed to escort Him and His angelic host back to the earth.

The noun *apantēsis* is found only three times in the New Testament. Besides I Thessalonians 4:17, it is used in Matthew 25:6 (in some manuscripts it is also found in verse 1), and Acts 28:15:

> Then shall the kingdom of heaven be likened unto ten virgins, which took their lamps, and went forth to meet the bridegroom. . . . And at midnight there was a cry made, Behold, the bridegroom cometh; go ye out to MEET [*apantēsis*] him (Matt. 25:1, 6).
>
> . . . And so we went toward Rome. And from thence, when the brethren heard of us, they came to MEET [*apantēsis*] us as far as Appii forum, and The three taverns (Acts 28:14b-15).

---

14. John Walvoord, *The Rapture Questions,* p. 205.
15. F. F. Bruce, *New Bible Commentary,* p. 1159.

In the parable of the ten virgins, which is clearly eschatological in nature, a direct parallel is made between an Oriental wedding and the Lord's return for His church. When the announcement of the bridegroom's arrival was sounded, the virgins arose and hurried out to meet the approaching bridegroom to escort him back to where they had been waiting. According to the Eastern wedding custom, the attendants to the bride (the virgins in the parable) went out from the bride's home to join the bridegroom's procession and accompany him back to his waiting bride. It would be ridiculous to imagine the virgins going out to greet the approaching bridegroom only to turn around and retreat to where he had come from. This would amount to an abrogation of the wedding ceremony. In this parable, the word "meet" (*apantēsis*) does not imply a reversal of direction.

The Acts account employing the word *apantēsis* describes an incident in the final leg of Paul's journey to Rome. The word "meet" is used in reference to a delegation of Roman Christians who rendezvoused with the Apostle Paul at Appii forum and then immediately proceeded to escort him to his intended destination of Rome. It does not suggest that Paul got as far as Appii forum, met the delegation of brethren, and then promptly returned with these brethren back to Caesarea from where the journey originated.

An honest examination of the distinctive usage of the word *apantēsis* conclusively demonstrates that it meant that as one party was making a journey (the Lord, the bridegroom, and the Apostle Paul), others came out to meet them, and then accompanied them to the end of their original destination without changing direction. Nowhere else in the scriptures is this word so used. It is consistently used to suggest the concept of an unimpeded advance in the same direction. In the case of I Thessalonians 4:17, that direction would be a descent of the Lord from heaven to earth.

In commenting upon the application of this unique word, Arthur Katterjohn added,

Another pretribulation distinctive is associated with the word "meet." It teaches that when we have met the Lord in the air, He will reverse direction, lead us back to heaven, and there we will pass the seven year period in which tribulation racks the earth. Does the word "meet" mean to change direction and return along the path just traveled? It is used only three times in Scripture: Matthew 25:6, Acts 28:15, and here

(I Thess. 4:17). . . . If the word "meet" in I Thessalonians 4:17 has essentially the same meaning as in the other two occurrences, then we get a picture of Christ descending to the earth, being met by His people in the air, and continuing down to set right the heresies of the tribulation. The saints, and not Christ, reverse direction. The Captain of the hosts does not retreat on His way to victory. He continues on.[16]

There isn't the slightest indication in the precise definition of the word *apantēsis* to suggest two stages of the Lord's return. Though the scriptures clearly reveal that the church will be caught up to "meet" the Lord in the air, it does not imply that we will return with Him to heaven to wait seven years before completing the second stage of His coming. By comprehending the unique manner in which the word "meet" is employed in the scriptures, we understand that when Christ comes, believers will be "caught up . . . to meet the Lord in the air," whereupon we will promptly accompany Him in His final victorious descent to earth. Thus, the second coming will be a coming which is both a time of coming "for" the saints, (as we ascend to meet Him in His earthward descent), and a coming "with" the saints (as we escort Him back to earth). Attempts to bolster the two-stage theory by placing a prolonged interval between Christ's coming "for" and coming "with" the saints has absolutely no scriptural basis. His coming "for" the saints at the rapture and His coming "with" the saints to earth are two aspects of a single, indivisible event—the Second Coming of Christ. This is the clear witness of scripture.

Why Do We Meet in the Air?

In spite of the argument that the word "meet" does not imply a reversal in direction, pretribulationists have difficulty understanding why the saints should have to rise to meet the Lord only to return immediately to the planet's surface. For example, Walvoord objected:

Actually, the posttribulationists do not have a good explanation of why it is necessary for the saints to leave the earth if, as a matter of fact, Christ is coming to the earth to reign on the earth.[17]

However, this objection poses no major difficulty for opponents of pretribulationism. The reason for the church ascending at the rapture

---

16. Arthur D. Katterjohn, *The Tribulation People*, p. 45.
17. John F. Walvoord, *The Rapture Question*, p. 206.

to meet the Lord and then return immediately to earth can be justified in a twofold manner. First of all we must ask, Why shouldn't the church be caught up to join the Lord in His glorious descent? Why shouldn't the church be granted the privilege of participating in the final glory of that triumphant occasion which she has eagerly anticipated for centuries? Secondly, we must take those rapture passages in context with the other second coming passages which couple the return of Christ for His people with the outpouring of divine judgment upon the wicked. This fact explains why God's people will be evacuated from the surface of the earth in conjunction with the awesome holocaust which will be suddenly unleashed upon an unregenerate humanity. Wilmot addresses the issue as follows:

> Indeed, these are the very conditions which explain the reason the church is to be caught up to meet the descending Lord. Why descend to the air at all if His objective were simply then to assemble His saints without respect to the other events? Why are they to be caught up to meet Him unless to join Him in His mighty undertaking? Why, if His object is to turn about from the air with them there and then to glory, to the Father's house; why not call them to His heavenly presence where He is enthroned and expecting? He Himself ascended up far above all heavens; Enoch and Elijah were taken up but He did not meet them halfway. The descent to the air warrants a reasonable explanation. It is in the day of wrath and righteous judgment from which believers have been delivered by virtue of His justifying substitute, and their identification with Him, that they shall be raptured to meet Him for Whom they wait. Thus "the saints shall judge the world."[18]

A final note on the word "descend" (*katabainō*) employed in I Thessalonians 4:16 is also helpful at this point. The word is consistently employed to characterize an uninterrupted descent. This is substantiated in those passages mentioning the descent of the Holy Spirit upon Christ at His baptism (Matt. 3:16; Mark 1:10; Luke 3:22; and John 1:32, 33). It is also borne out in passages which refer to Christ's first advent (John 3:13; 6:38, 41, 42, 50, 51, 58). It is also employed numerous times in the New Testament in which its context clearly states or suggests an uninterrupted descent. When a change of direction in the descent is stated, a specific statement is included to

---

18. John Wilmot, *Inspired Principles of Interpretation,* p. 194.

qualify it. Furthermore, the pretribulational contention that the phrase "We . . . shall be caught up . . . in the clouds to meet the Lord in the air: AND SO SHALL WE EVER BE WITH THE LORD" (I Thess. 4:17) is proof that the saints will go to heaven for several years before returning to the earth is an anemic one at best. This phrase was not intended to mean that we will remain with the Lord in the clouds for seven years. If this was the case, pretribulationists would be in a confusing dilemma, simply because the phrase states "so shall we EVER BE with the Lord." If anything, this argument would imply that the church will never return to earth but remain hovering in the clouds forever. However, the obvious intended meaning of this verse is that at the time of the rapture, when saints are changed in the "twinkling of an eye" and gloriously transformed from mortality to immortality, we will enter an intimate, consummated relationship with the Lord Jesus Christ which will last for eternity.

8

Terminology of the Second Coming

The writers of the New Testament employ several key words to describe the second coming. The precise application of these words has formed the repeated battleground for many a conflict between pretribulationists and their opponents. Proponents of the two-stage coming perspective commonly teach that a study of the original Greek application of these terms demonstrates a distinct manner in which these words are applied to the specific stages of Christ's return.

A Definition of Terms

The following Greek words are used to describe the various aspects of Christ's return:

1. *Parousia* - This word is usually translated "coming." It is used to denote the actual personal presence of one who comes or arrives. It is employed in a number of eschatological passages (i.e., Matt. 24:3, 27, 37, 39; I Cor. 15:23; I Thess. 2:19; 3:13; 4:15; 5:23; II Thess. 2:1; 2:8; James 5:7, 8; II Peter 1:16; II Peter 3:4, 12; I John 2:28).

135

2. *Apokalupsis* - This word literally means "an unveiling, uncovering, or appearing." It is translated "appearing, revelation, and manifestation." It is used to characterize the open appearing or manifestation of Christ at His second coming (see Rom. 8:19; I Cor. 1:7; II Thess. 1:7; I Peter 1:7, 13; 4:13).

3. *Epiphaneia* - This word literally means "a shining forth or displaying." It is where we derive our English word "epiphany" which means "an appearance or manifestation—especially of a divine person." It is employed in the New Testament in reference to the manifestation of glory which will accompany Christ's coming. It is translated "appearing" in those passages pertaining to the second coming (Matt. 24:27; II Thess. 2:8; I Tim. 6:14; II Tim. 4:1, 8; Titus 2:13).

4. *Phaneroo* - This word means "to make visible, clear, manifest, known, to lay bare, to reveal, and to uncover." It aptly characterizes the visible, public return of Christ. It is translated "manifest" or "appear" (I Peter 5:4; I John 2:28; 3:2).

The Greek language is colorful and exacting in its ability to capture and communicate subtle shades of thought. These terms were employed under the divine guidance of the Holy Spirit to depict the various aspects of Christ's second coming; but none of these terms lend support to the common pretribulational contention that there will be two distinct phases of the Lord's advent separated by several years. The employment of these terms strongly substantiates the conclusion that the coming of Christ will be a single, indivisible event which synchronizes the return of Christ in judgment and glory with the rapture and the translation of the church.

A Common Pretrib Position

In spite of the fact that they are consistently used in an interchangeable and integrated manner to describe the one and selfsame coming of Christ, many pretribulationists continue to insist upon restricting the application of these terms to either the secret rapture or the public appearance of Christ in judgment and glory. This is often done with the word *parousia* by arguing that it lends itself to the secret, personal appearance of Christ for His people rather than His public appearance at the end of the age. The following pretribulational quote is representative of the pretrib position embraced by many:

136

The two phases of Christ's second coming are clearly distinguished in the Greek. The "parousia" . . . is his coming for his saints . . . the "apokalupsis" (the revealing, unveiling, making manifest) is his coming with his saints.[1]

In referring to the parousia, Dake stated:

> This refers to the rapture, not the second advent of Christ. It is the same as in I Thessalonians 3:13; 4:13-17. . . . These two comings should not be confused. The scriptures that apply to one do not apply to the other. Not one passage refers to both events as if they were one.[2]

In contrasting the application of the parousia and His open revelation, Darby asserted that,

> The church's joining Christ has nothing to do with Christ's appearing or coming to earth.[3]

However, contrary to such pretrib assertions, a careful examination of the vocabulary used to describe the Lord's return reveals that these various terms are used in a harmonious fashion to prove the reality of only one second coming of Christ. The New Testament does not support the pretrib distinction between the rapture event and the return of Christ. As Allis noted:

> The question which confronts us is this. If the distinction between the rapture and the appearing is of as great moment as Dispensationalists assert, how are we to explain Paul's failure to distinguish clearly between them? And the failure of other writers, Peter, James and John, to do the same? Paul was a logician. He was able to draw sharp distinctions. If he had wanted, or regarded it important, to distinguish between these events, he could have done so very easily. Why did he use language which Dispensationalists must admit to be confusing? . . . If the distinction is negligible, accuracy of statement would be quite unnecessary. We conclude, therefore, that the usage of the New Testament and especially Paul not merely fails to prove the distinction insisted on by Dispensationalists but rather by its very ambiguity indicates clearly and unmistakably that no such distinction exists.[4]

---

1. Carl Sabiers, *Where Are the Dead?* pp. 123, 124.
2. J. Finis Dake, *Dake's Annotated Reference Bible,* p. 227.
3. John N. Darby, *The Rapture & Collected Writings XI,* p. 233.
4. Oswald T. Allis, *Prophecy and the Church,* pp. 184-185.

When commenting upon the terminology of the second coming, Charles Feinberg, a noted dispensationalist, also candidly confessed:

> We conclude, then, that from a study of the Greek words themselves the distinction between the coming of the Lord for His saints and with His saints is not to be gleaned.[5]

This forthright admission helps demonstrate the weakness in attempting to establish a valid scriptural distinction between the phases of Christ's return, based on terminology.

The "Parousia"

The primary word appealed to by pretribulationists to support a two phase coming is the Greek word "parousia." It is found in the key rapture text of I Thessalonians:

> For this we say unto you by the word of the Lord, that we which are alive and remain unto the COMING [*parousia*] of the Lord shall not prevent them which are asleep. For the Lord himself shall descend from heaven with a shout, with the voice of the archangel, with the trump of God: and the dead in Christ shall rise first: Then we which are alive and remain shall be caught up together with them in the clouds, to meet the Lord in the air (I Thess. 4:15-17).

Pretribulationists repeatedly stress that the word *parousia* refers to Christ's secret personal arrival for His church at the rapture. They claim that it characterizes His mysterious presence in conjunction with His celestial rendezvous with His people rather than His open, glorious appearance before the entire world at the day of judgment. However, as I have repeatedly emphasized, this supposed secret rapture proof text suggests anything but a mysterious, invisible, silent coming of Christ. As LaRondelle commented:

> No trace of a secret, invisible, or instantaneous rapture of the church is to be found in the New Testament. On the contrary, I Thessalonians 4:15-17 suggests the very opposite. . . . No word about secrecy, or invisibility, or even about an instantaneous rapture is found here. Paul, in I Corinthians 15, reveals the mystery that the church will be "changed" from mortality to immortality "in a flash, in the twinkling of an eye, at the last trumpet" (verse 52). It is this transformation that will be

5. Charles L. Feinberg, *Premillennialism or Amillennialism?* p. 207.

instantaneous, according to Paul, not the rapture from the earth to the air or to heaven. The parousia of Christ will be the most dramatic, earthshaking event in human history.[6]

The word *parousia* was a familiar one to the average Greek reader of Paul's day. It was not a rarely used word. This has been repeatedly demonstrated through the archaeological discoveries of the last one hundred years which have unearthed many examples of the word in the papyri documents of the Middle East. When expounding upon the contemporary understanding and usage of the word *parousia* at the time of the early church, Deissman noted:

> From the Ptolemaic period down into the 2nd century A.D. we are able to trace the word in the East as a technical expression for the arrival or the visit of the king or emperor (or other persons in authority, or troops). The parousia of the sovereign must have been something well known even to the people, as shown by the facts that special payments in kind and taxes to defray the cost of the parousia were exacted, that in Greece a new era was reckoned from the parousia of the Emperor Hadrian, that all over the world advent-coins were struck after a parousia of the emperor, and that we are even able to quote examples of advent sacrifices.[7]

So common was the term that the Greek-speaking world of the first century would have had little difficulty comprehending its intended meaning and application. As Reese observed:

> Parousia was everywhere used in the sense of the arrival or coming of kings and rulers on a visit. How appropriate to the arrival of our Saviour-God, Jesus Christ, when He comes in triumph. . . .[8]

To this Moffatt added:

> On the lips of the Greek-speaking Christians in the primitive church parousia was almost exclusively applied to the return of Christ in glory in order to complete the Messianic work and usher in the Final Judgment.[9]

---

6. Hans K. LaRondelle, *The Israel of God in Prophecy,* p. 188.

7. Adolf Deissman, *Light From the Ancient East,* cited from *The Approaching Advent of Christ,* p. 145.

8. Alexander Reese, *The Approaching Advent of Christ,* p. 150.

9. James Moffatt, *Hastings Encyclopedia of Religion and Ethics, Vol. 9,* p. 637.

A careful study of the historical application of the word *parousia*, especially at the writing of Paul's epistles, shows that there is nothing inherent in this regal term to suggest the idea of secrecy, certainly not to the typical Greek reader in Paul's day. On this point Murray commented:

> The early Christians knew very well what was involved in the parousia of the emperor. They too had a king-emperor whom they expected to come and they were making preparation for His parousia. . . . We can well imagine the thoughts passing through the minds of those suffering Christians in the early church as they read in Paul's letters of the parousia of their Lord. They probably witnessed the parousia of a Roman emperor with all its pomp, and its tokens and trophies of conquest. There was a parousia yet to come in which they were to be given signal recognition and in the joys of which they were to participate. It is, however, difficult to see how the theory of a "secret coming," and that only "part of the way" could be based upon the word parousia, the arrival of the king. This unwarranted twisting of Scripture can hardly be expected to further the interests of truth.[10]

The word *parousia* simply characterizes the bodily, personal presence of one who has come or arrived, particularly in respect to a person of dignity or rank. It implies nothing about the secret nature of that arrival. For example, Paul spoke of being comforted by the "coming [*parousia*] of Titus" (II Cor. 7:6) and the "coming [*parousia*] of Stephanas and Fortunatus and Achaicus" (I Cor. 16:17).

Not only is the parousia of Christ inseparably linked to the rapture of the church and the resurrection of the righteous dead in Christ, but it is also associated with the time when the Man of sin is destroyed:

> And then shall that Wicked be revealed, whom the Lord shall consume with the spirit of his mouth, and shall destroy with the brightness of his COMING [*parousia*] (II Thess. 2:8).

Contrary to the assertions of many pretribulationists, this verse clearly indicates that the parousia will be an awesome day of judgment as well as relief for the church.

In parallel manner, we find further evidence in II Peter proving that the parousia is not a secret, mysterious evacuation of the church seven years prior to Christ's coming in judgment. According to the

---

10. George L. Murray, *Millennial Studies*, p. 134.

apostle Peter, "The promise of his coming [*parousia*]" will be consummated upon a scoffing world when "the day of the Lord will come as a thief in the night; in the which the heavens shall pass away with a great noise, and the elements shall melt with fervent heat" (II Peter 3:4-10). In the immediate context of this revelation, Peter exhorts us to be "looking for and hasting unto the coming [*parousia*] of the day of God, wherein the heavens being on fire shall be dissolved, and the elements shall melt with fervent heat" (II Peter 3:11, 12). A candid examination of these facts conclusively demonstrates that the word parousia has nothing whatsoever to do with a supposed secret presence, arrival, or appearance of Christ in the form of an invisible rapture.

Even in Christ's personal characterization of His return, He emphasized that it would be a glorious, public parousia:

> For as the lightning cometh out of the east, and shineth even unto the west; so shall also the coming [*parousia*] of the Son of man be (Matt. 24:27).

From Christ's own statements regarding His return, we see that the parousia will be a visible, bold, and dramatic event similar to a sudden bolt of lightning. There is nothing in His description of the parousia to suggest the secret nature of this event. In fact, this is precisely what Christ was striving to protect His followers from assuming. As Fletcher noted:

> In order to guard believers against this very idea of a Secret Rapture, Christ taught His disciples, "If they shall say unto you, Behold, he is in the desert; go not forth: behold, he is in the SECRET CHAMBERS; believe it not. For as the lightning cometh out of the East, and SHINETH even unto the West, so (visible) shall also the coming (parousia) of the Son of man be" (Matt. 24:26, 27). Hence, as the lightning flash is open and visible to all, so is Christ's coming (PAROUSIA) to be.[11]

It should be further emphasized that this lucid caution of Christ completely undermines the pretribulational defense of a secret rapture, and that His statement was purposefully designed to warn the entire church age of just that:

---

11. George B. Fletcher, *Will a Secret Rapture Precede the Second Coming of Christ?* p. 2.

He is cautioning Christians of all ages not to be swayed by deceptive teachings which claim that Christ's coming will be characterized by silence or subtly. He flatly rejects the concept that His appearance will be somehow cloaked in secrecy. Too often in the history of the church, elements within the Christian community have been foolishly misled by either the blatant delusions of spiritual quacks, or the imbalanced and misguided instructions of good-intentioned Christians concerning the characteristics of the Lord's return. The Christian's credulity and gullibility have often been played upon by those who have implied that the Lord's return would be secret and mysterious.[12]

The *"Apokalupsis"*

Another strategic word in reference to the Lord's coming is the Greek word *apokalupsis*. Many pretribulationists distinguish the apocalypse, or the open revelation of Christ, from the rapture of the church at the parousia. They place the apokalupsis at the end of the age when Christ comes in glory and judgment. As Scofield affirmed:

The word emphasizes the visibility of the Lord's return. It is used of the Lord (II Thess. 1:7; I Peter 1:7, 13; 4:13), of the sons of God in connection with the Lord's return . . . and always implies perceptibility.[13]

While not agreeing that the parousia refers to the subtle appearance of Christ at the rapture, both pre and posttribulationists would agree that the apokalupsis will transpire at the time when God unleashes His final judgments at His public return.

Pretribulationists claim that the secret rapture is what Christians are to be eagerly anticipating and longing for and not the open, public manifestation or revelation of Christ. However, this is not in harmony with the obvious statements of scripture. For example, in I Corinthians 1:7 Paul informs us that we are "waiting for the coming [*apokalupsis*] of our Lord Jesus Christ." According to the clear thrust of this passage, the church is not waiting for a secret, mysterious arrival of Christ, but for His public, visible manifestation. This scriptural

---

12. William R. Kimball, *What the Bible Says About the Great Tribulation*, p. 145.
13. Cyrus I. Scofield, *Scofield Reference Bible*, pp. 1232, 1233.

fact completely contradicts the pretribulationist's infatuation with a secret rapture expectation.

As I have previously indicated, Christians are instructed that we will weather the pangs of affliction until the time when Christ comes to provide relief and to inflict retribution upon the ungodly. The scriptures reveal that this will transpire at the apokalupsis:

> Seeing it is a righteous thing with God to recompense tribulation to them that trouble you; And to you who are troubled rest with us, when the Lord Jesus shall be REVEALED [*apokalupsis*] from heaven with his mighty angels, in flaming fire taking vengeance on them that know not God, and that obey not the gospel of our Lord Jesus Christ: Who shall be punished with everlasting destruction from the presence of the Lord, and from the glory of his power; When he shall come to be glorified in his saints, and to be admired in all them that believe (because our testimony among you was believed) in that day (II Thess. 1:6-10).

According to the pretribulational scheme of end-time events, the actual "rest" from affliction is slated to occur at a secret rapture seven years before the public revelation (apokalupsis) of Christ. But in spite of the complicated twisting and exegetical gymnastics to the contrary, this text is straightforward in its assertion that our "rest" is received at Christ's apokalupsis, and not before. Regarding this fact, Reese questioned:

> Could Paul have written this passage if he believed that Christians are to be raptured away to heaven several years or decades before the Day of the Lord comes? The suggestion is fantastic. Once it is seen that the "rest" is a noun, the object of "recompense," then Darby's scheme falls like a house of cards. He and his associates and followers have a comforting scheme that the Elect will be raptured away several years before the day of Judgment described in this chapter. Yet Paul, dealing specifically with the question of relief from tribulation, says that Christians will get it "at the Revelation of the Lord Jesus from heaven with the angels of his power in flaming fire, rendering vengeance to them that know not God, and to them that obey not the gospel" (R.V.).[14]

Peter also provides the same parallel instruction concerning the termination of our sufferings:

---

14. Alexander Reese, *The Approaching Advent of Christ*, p. 135, 136.

> But rejoice, inasmuch as ye are partakers of Christ's sufferings; that, when his glory shall be REVEALED [*apokalupsis*], ye may be glad also with exceeding joy (I Peter 4:13).

This statement again indicates that our fiery trials will ultimately cease at the apokalupsis of Christ.

Peter further reveals that the precious quality of a Christian's faith which has endured trying will "be found unto praise and honour and glory at the appearing [*apokalupsis*] of Jesus Christ" (I Peter 1:7). But according to pretribulational dogma, this glory, honor, and praise will have already been experienced by believers seven years prior to Christ's "appearing" at a secret rapture. However, it is the intended objective of this verse to comfort Christians by establishing the truth that one of the beneficial purposes of Christ's apokalupsis is to bring to His people glory and honor and praise because of their steadfastness in their faith.

Peter also addresses the public revelation of Christ in I Peter 1:13:

> Wherefore gird up the loins of your mind, be sober, and hope to the end for the grace that is to be brought unto you at the REVELATION [*apokalupsis*] of Jesus Christ.

The obvious implication of this statement is that the rapture is not an event which will take place seven years before the revelation. If this had been the case, then Peter's instructions about being sober and hoping until the revelation (apokalupsis) of Christ would be meaningless. It would be pointless for believers to hope to the end for the grace that is to be brought unto us at the revelation of Christ if, in reality, this grace is brought to us at a secret rapture seven years earlier.

An honest examination of the word "apokalupsis" shows that it is what Christians are waiting for, hoping for, and when we will ultimately be delivered from the sufferings of this present age. It is apparent from the context in which the word is employed that the rapture and the revelation are not two separate events. Instead of two distinct stages of Christ's coming being clearly distinguished in the Greek, the terms *parousia* and *apokalupsis* reveal that both are used interchangeably to characterize the one and only second coming of Christ.

144

The "Epiphaneia"

Another prominent word used to describe the return of Christ is the Greek word *epiphaneia*. As we have seen, the word refers to the manisfestation of shining forth in glory that will accompany the Lord when He comes. The fact that it means manifestation prevents it from being applied to the pretribulational notion of a secret, silent, mysterious rapture. The proof that it contains no reference to a secret pretrib rapture can be seen in II Thessalonians 2:8 where we read that Christ will slay the Man of sin "with the brightness [*epiphaneia*] of his coming [*parousia*]." What is even more conclusive is the fact that not only is the word [*epiphaneia*] used in conjunction with Christ's coming in judgment, but it is also intimately associated with Christ's *parousia*—an event which is scripturally linked to Christ's coming for His people. As Fletcher pointed out:

> "And then shall the Wicked (the man of sin) be revealed, whom the Lord shall consume with the spirit of his mouth, and shall DESTROY with the (EPIPHANEIA TEES PAROUSIAS AUTOU) brightness of his coming." Here both words are applied to one action, EPIPHANEIA being rendered "brightness" and PAROUSIA, "coming." This passage proves first, that the PAROUSIA and EPIPHANEIA are simultaneous; and, second, that the career of "the man of sin" ENDS (instead of begins) at the PAROUSIA, when the saints are delivered, and does not extend to a subsequent EPIPHANEIA, as the secret rapture theorists teach.[15]

The manner in which they are so contextually sandwiched together in this verse lends little room for the notion of a lengthy interval between the *parousia* and the *epiphaneia*. As Thomas added, "Here we have two words and it is impossible to put seven years between them. To make two separate comings of the Lord Jesus Christ with an interlude of seven years is the height of folly."[16]

In I Timothy, another key passage argues forcefully against a pretrib rapture:

> I give thee charge in the sight of God, who quickeneth all things, and before Christ Jesus . . . that thou keep this commandment without

15. George B. Fletcher, *Will a Secret Rapture Precede the Second Coming of Christ?* p. 6.
16. Lawrence R. Thomas, *Does the Bible Teach Millennialism?* p. 81.

spot, unrebukeable, until the APPEARING [*epiphaneia*] of our Lord Jesus Christ (I Tim. 6:13, 14).

In light of these verses, one should question why Paul would exhort us to "keep this commandment" until the *epiphaneia* (the glorious appearing and manifestation) if the rapture of the church is scheduled to occur in a subtle manner seven years before His glorious appearing.

At the conclusion of Paul's earthly sojourn, he delivered his victorious epitaph to the church in which he declares his confidence that he had "fought the good fight" (II Tim. 4:7). He then added:

> Henceforth there is laid up for me a crown of righteousness, which the Lord, the righteous judge, shall give me at that day: and not to me only, but unto ALL THEM also that love his APPEARING [*epiphaneia*] (II Tim. 4:8).

Paul pinpoints the precise day of rewards (crown of righteousness) as the day of appearing (epiphaneia). We can confidently glean from Paul's declaration that "that day" of anticipated reward will be none other than the glorious epiphany of Christ. This is clearly the day that Paul had set his affections upon, and the same day which he revealed as the earnest hope of "all those who love his appearing." However, according to pretribulational teaching, the real day of rewards will transpire just after the rapture, which is years before the open revelation (epiphaneia and apokalupsis) of Christ.

In the immediate context of this statement, Paul also informs us that this day of Christ's appearing will not only be a time when believers are rewarded with crowns of righteousness but it will also be the day when the ungodly are judged:

> I charge thee therefore before God, and the Lord Jesus Christ, who shall judge the quick and the dead at his APPEARING [*epiphaneia*] and his kingdom. (II Tim. 4:1).

In Titus 2:13 Paul further reveals that the church is to be,

> Looking for that blessed hope, and the GLORIOUS APPEARING [*epiphaneia*] of the great God and our Saviour Jesus Christ.

Paul's wording clearly informs us that the "blessed hope" which we are looking for is Christ's spectacular, open, visible appearance and manifestation, and not a subtle, silent, mysterious appearance seven years prior. The real "blessed hope" of believers is the glorious

146

appearing of Christ—His epiphany. This fact completely undermines the concept that the Church is, in reality, looking for a secret rapture seven years before His glorious public manifestation.

> And a man half-asleep can see that modern scholarship's contribution at Titus ii. 13 spells ruin, and the irretrievable ruin, of pre-tribs' comforting programme of the End. For according to them "the blessed hope" is a secret event, clean detached from all connexion with the Day of the Lord, which, they tell us, is a terrible and terrifying affair, occurring several years . . . later, whereas according to Paul the blessed hope of Christians is none other than the Glorious Appearing itself.[17]

From a careful survey of the Greek word *epiphaneia* we can safely conclude that it is a day in which the "man of sin" is destroyed; it is the time of Christ's glorious appearing, it is the time when the faithful will be rewarded with crowns of righteousness; it is the time of God's judgment; it is until this time that Christians are exhorted to remain faithful; and it is the day of "blessed hope" which believers are to be looking for and earnestly anticipating.

The "Phaneroo"

The fourth and final word in our list of terms applying to the second advent is the Greek word *phaneroo* which means "to be made apparent, or evident, or manifest." Vine added this enlightening qualification when defining the word *phaneroo*:

> To be manifested, in the Scriptural sense of the word, is more than to appear. A person may appear in a false guise or without a disclosure of what he truly is; to be manifested is to be revealed in one's true character; this is especially the meaning of phaneroo.[18]

The word, by its very definition, can carry no conceivable reference to a secret, obscure, mysterious, concealed appearing of Christ.

In I Peter we read:

> And when the chief Shepherd shall APPEAR [*phaneroo*], ye shall receive a crown of glory that fadeth not away (I Peter 5:4).

Peter's revelation closely parallels that of Paul's in II Timothy 4:8. The contextual similarities in which phaneroo and epiphaneia are

---

17. Alexander Reese, *The Approaching Advent of Christ*, p. 129.
18. W. E. Vine, *Expository Dictionary of New Testament Words*, p. 65.

employed in connection with the time when Christians will be crowned cannot be dismissed lightly. Neither can their association to the glorious day of Christ's return be easily ignored.

Not only will the phaneroo of the Lord be the time when Christians will be crowned, but it will also be the time when we will be gloriously changed to be like Him:

> But we know that, when he shall APPEAR [*phaneroo*], we shall be like him; for we shall see him as he is (I John 3:2b).

The Apostle John makes it quite evident that when Christ appears, we will be changed into His likeness. This revelation is compatible with Paul's rapture characterization in I Corinthians 15:51-54. This transformation will occur at Christ's glorious appearing, and not at a subtle, hidden rapture.

The "Bema"

Pretribulationists occasionally contend that there must be an adequate interval of time between the rapture of the church and the public manifestation of Christ in order for Christians to receive their rewards at the judgment seat (bema) of Christ. They differentiate between the judgment seat of Christ (Rom. 14:10; II Cor. 5:10) and the Great White Throne Judgment in Revelation 20:11. They claim that the bema (I Cor. 3:15) will be a judgment of rewards for the righteous which will convene immediately after the parousia of Christ and the rapture of the church. For example, when touching upon the word *bema*, Vine injects his pretribulational bias as follows:

> The judgment-seat of Christ will be a tribunal held in "His Parousia," i.e., His presence with His saints after His return to receive them to Himself.[19]

They place this time of judgment between the rapture and the open appearing of Christ at the end of the age. As Pentecost affirmed, ". . . it must be observed that the rewarding of the church must take place between the rapture and the revelation of Christ to the earth."[20]

However, the pretribulational supposition that the saints must be rewarded prior to Christ's return in glory is based upon pure conjecture.

---

19. W. E. Vine, *Expository Dictionary of New Testament Words,* p. 283.
20. J. Dwight Pentecost, *Things to Come,* p. 221.

148

The Bible says absolutely nothing about a prior judgment of rewards before Christ's final coming. Ladd raised this perceptive question regarding this issue:

> . . . if a period of time must intervene for this judgment to take place, will seven years be enough? It is estimated that there are two hundred million living Christians [not counting the millions who have already died in Christ]. In seven years, there are just over two hundred million seconds. How much of a fraction of a second is necessary for the judgment of each believer? If an interval of time is needed, then far more than seven years is required.[21]

In light of this objection, the pretribulational argument demanding a sufficient time span of seven years to dispense rewards falls flat. Just how much of a fraction of a second is necessary to be alloted to each individual believer? If, as Pentecost claims, "This is an individual judgment of each believer before the Lord,"[22] how will seven years possibly provide adequate time for the hundreds of millions of saints who will personally appear before the bema of Christ?

Interchangeability

A careful review of these Greek words demonstrates that they are employed in a harmonious and interchangeable manner in referring to and characterizing the second coming, and not to two stages of the second coming. For example, the words *parousia* and *apokalupsis* are used interchangeably in the two parallel references to the days of Noah:

> But as the days of Noe were, so shall also the COMING [*parousia*] of the Son of man be (Matt. 24:37).

> And as it was in the days of Noe . . . . Even thus shall it be in the day when the Son of man is REVEALED [*apokalupto*, akin to *apokalupsis*] (Luke 17:26, 30).

This contextual comparison reveals that the words *parousia* and *apokalupsis* are used interchangeably in reference to the same event.

The words *parousia* and *epiphaneia* are also linked together in II Thessalonians 2:8 where we read that the Wicked One will be

---

21. George E. Ladd, *The Blessed Hope,* p. 103.
22. J. Dwight Pentecost, *Things to Come,* p. 223.

destroyed by the "BRIGHTNESS" (epiphaneia) of the Lord's "COMING" (parousia). What is more, the words *parousia* and *phaneroo* are joined together in reference to the same event:

> And now, little children, abide in him; that when he shall APPEAR [*phaneroo*], we may have confidence, and not be ashamed before him at his COMING [*parousia*] (I John 2:28).

In conclusion, the corroborative evidence strongly defends the reality that these various terms are used interchangeably in characterizing the same event. Though each of these words possess shades of meaning, they lend absolutely no support to the pretribulational distinction in phases of the second coming. As LaRondelle noted:

> We arrive, therefore, at the conclusion that the New Testament makes no distinction between the parousia, the apocalupsis, and the epiphaneia of Jesus Christ. These terms signify one single, indivisible advent of Christ to bring salvation and glorious immortality to all believers, and judgment to their wicked persecutors.[23]

The parousia, the apokalupsis (apocalypse), the epiphaneia (epiphany), and the phaneroo all occur simultaneously in depicting the same event. As Cox concluded:

> One can readily see that these terms . . . portray synonymous concepts, and that they refer to a singular event. These different terms are used, not to depict different occasions, but rather to draw attention to unique aspects of that one great occasion. Each is simply a different facet of a single gem. In one context the inspired writer intended to emphasize the certainty of Jesus' coming; another writer wished to elucidate the fact that our Lord's majesty—which is presently hidden from view— will be revealed at his second coming; another text will bring comfort to the believer as he is reminded that our Lord will some day be bodily present and that his appearing will be visible for all to behold.[24]

Any attempt to apply these words to different stages or divisions of Christ's return constitutes an unwarranted wrenching of scriptures from their context. The terminology of the second coming provides no support for the notion of two phases of Christ's return. On the contrary, they conclusively substantiate the contention that the Lord's

---

23. Hans K. LaRondelle, *The Israel of God in Prophecy*, p. 188.
24. William E. Cox, *Biblical Studies in Final Things*, p. 119.

return will be one, glorious, public, and indivisible event which will terminate this age and mark the time when the church will finally enter our consummated relationship with the Lord.

An Objection Considered

While many pretribulational advocates restrict the application of such terms as the parousia and the apokalupsis to either the secret rapture or the visible return of Christ, an increasing number have come to reject this view. The reasons for this defection lie in direct proportion to the amount of study devoted to the actual New Testament application of these terms.

Many pretribulationists have come to recognize the inherent weaknesses in trying to restrict the application of these words. Attempts to limit the designation of these terms to a specific phase of the Lord's return have not stood up to the acid test of scripture. A careful examination of New Testament usage conclusively demonstrates that these terms are not referring to two distinct stages of the second advent.

Though many readily admit that the terms are used interchangeably in reference to the rapture and the glorious appearing of Christ, they strongly object to the technical meaning conveyed through these words. Some pretribulationists unconditionally reject the technical designation of these terms by retreating into a maze of generalizations. This is especially true when the terms distinguish the timing of the rapture and pinpoint it as the one and only second coming of Christ. They must relegate the intended meaning of these terms to irrelevance or be forced to admit that the "blessed hope" of the church is indeed the glorious appearing (epiphaneia) of Christ and not a secret rapture. They must play down the technical designation or be forced to admit that the church really is waiting for the open, public, glorious revelation (apokalupsis) of Christ and not a secret, silent rapture.

But pretribulational arguments invariably reveal their inconsistency and confusion on the issue of terminology. For example, while Ryrie can generalize on the one hand that, "the vocabulary used in the New Testament does not seem to prove either pre or posttribulationism,"[25] he executes a flip-flop in concluding his defense by answering his

---

25. Charles C. Ryrie, *What You Should Know About the Rapture*, p. 45.

151

own question: "Do presence, revelation, and manifestation character-ize different events, or catalogue the same event? The pretribulationist says the former, the posttribulationist the later."[26] It seems that they are willing to adopt specific characterizations of these terms when it suits their two-phase theory, but ardently challenge any attempts of their opponents to do otherwise.

While contending that these terms are not technical expressions used to characterize various facets of the second coming, pretribulationists consistently do a reversal by claiming that these terms can make a definite distinction based upon the context. However, their appeal to context is a weak one at best and one built on both a faulty exegesis and a totally arbitrary application of the terms. It is only employed when it serves pretrib purposes or lends a convenient support to their attempts to establish a distinction between the pretrib rapture and the public appearing of Christ. The ultimate determination of whether a term applies to one event or to the other is left to the purely arbitrary bias of the interpreter—certainly not the principles of sound hermeneu-tics. In spite of their defense of interchangeability and their argument that these terms neither support pre or posttribulationism, pretribula-tionists inevitably end up with a self-imposed application of the terms and a form of interpretive, situational ethics which suits them best when attempting to defend a two-phase theory.

---

26. Ibid., pp. 46, 47.

9

The Day of the Lord

A distinction is often made between the "day of Christ" and the "day of the Lord." Pretribulationists associate the "day of Christ" with the time of blessing and reward for God's people at the rapture of the church. They distinguish this day from the "day of the Lord" which they restrict to the time of apocalyptic judgment which will engulf the ungodly at Christ's public return. For example, Scofield presented this position as follows:

> The "day of Christ" relates wholly to the reward and blessing of saints at His coming, as "day of the Lord" is connected with judgment.[1]

Two Views

However, not all pretribulationists agree on the timing element associated with the "day of the Lord." Basically, there are two views.

---

1. Cyrus I. Scofield, *Scofield Reference Bible,* p. 1212, note 2.

The older view holds that the "day of the Lord" commences with the return of Christ in judgment at the end of the tribulation and extends until the consummation of the climactic events at the end of the millennial reign. Scofield outlined this view as follows:

> The day of Jehovah (called also "that day" and "the great day") is that lengthened period of time beginning with the return of the Lord in glory, and ending with the purgation of the heavens and the earth by fire preparatory to the new heavens and the new earth.[2]

However, in time many came to recognize the inherent weaknesses in the older view, chiefly, the claim that the "day of the Lord" will come as a thief in the night in a sudden and unexpected manner after the catastrophic events of a final tribulation period. This presented an irreconcilable contradiction which has forced many contemporary pretribulationists to extend the time frame of the "day of the Lord" to include the entire tribulation period. As a consequence, noted individuals such as Pentecost, Ryrie, and Walvoord have adopted the more recent view which basically stretches the "day of the Lord" to include a seven year tribulation period commencing immediately after the pretrib rapture of the church. As Pentecost affirmed:

> . . . it is sufficient to point out that the term Day of the Lord, or that day, is not a term which applies to a twenty-four hour period, but rather the whole program of events, including the tribulation period, the second advent program, and the entire millennial age. It may be said to be that of the whole period beginning with the judgments of the seventieth week and extending through the millennial age.[3]

Based on Inference

But opponents of this perspective reject this elastic interpretation on the grounds that it is based upon inference. They maintain that pretribulationists have adopted this convenient expedient in order to reconcile their position to the glaring objections of scriptural reality. They hold that pretribulationists have simply utilized this exegetical maneuver in order to rescue their original position and conform the scriptures to their prophetic system. As Carver pointed out:

---

2. Ibid., p. 1349, note 1.
3. J. Dwight Pentecost, *Things to Come,* p. 174.

It is obviously an interpretation stretched to fit in with the difficulties of a theory that leaks in a thousand places. That the Day of the Lord is a period of Time we will not dispute; but that it is a combination of three periods (The Glorious Advent, the Millennium, and then the final destruction of creation, with the final Judgment set up) is gross extravagance generated by unscriptural speculation. Of course, even Scofield's interpretation has been stretched further by present-day theorists, and "the Day" now commences not at the "revelation," but at the beginning of "the great tribulation." Space is precious, but we must draw the line somewhere in seeking to follow the vagaries of these ever-changing speculations; hence this is not the place to try and sort out these folk. We are satisfied that the historic interpretation that "the Coming," and "the Day of the Lord" are the great Day of His Appearing, is correct.[4]

The Same Day

Opponents of this pretribulational position generally maintain that the "day of the Lord" and the "day of Christ" are synonymous and occur at the glorious second coming of Christ for His church at the end of this age. They claim that there is no scriptural justification for distinguishing a difference between these two days. As Sisco stated:

To make the day of Christ the time of the rapture, the time of reward and blessing of the saints apart from judgment; to make the day of the Lord a lengthened period of time (1007 years) ending with the purgation of the heavens and the earth by fire, the day of God, is to be carried about with divers and strange doctrines . . . the day of the Lord and the day of God are not separate or different events or periods of time as Scofield says. They are synonymous.[5]

Objections to the pretribulational distinction between the "day of the Lord" and the "day of Christ" are based upon strong appeals to the scriptures. Paul confirms this in a number of key passages. For example, in I Corinthians we read:

So that ye come behind in no gift; waiting for the COMING [apokalupsis] OF OUR LORD JESUS CHRIST: Who shall also confirm you UNTO THE

---

4. Arthur Carver, *The Great Consummation,* p. 74.
5. Paul E. Sisco, *Scofield or the Scriptures,* pp. 61, 63.

END, that ye may be blameless in the DAY OF OUR LORD JESUS CHRIST (I Cor. 1:7, 8).

In this verse, Paul draws no distinction between the "day of Christ" and the "day of the Lord." The phrase, "DAY of our LORD Jesus CHRIST" combines both the day of the Lord and the day of Christ. These verses also associate that day with the glorious coming (apocalypse) of Christ, and reveal that it is Paul's earnest desire that we be confirmed "UNTO THE END." He characterizes this end as both the "day of Christ" and the "day of the Lord." They were synonymous as far as Paul was concerned. If he had understood them as referring to different days or had intended any distinction at all, he would not have run the risk of confusing his readers or hopelessly misleading them by combining these phrases.

This point is also paralleled in I Corinthians 5:5 and II Corinthians 1:14 where Paul combines the day of the Lord with the day of Jesus (see also Phil. 1:6, 10; 2:16). The variant designations which he uses in reference to that day clearly indicate that no difference existed in his mind. As Neilson noted:

> The different designations of day are only different terms for essentially the same day. . . . I would have extreme difficulty just from a language standpoint in asserting that the day of our Lord Jesus Christ is different from the day of the Lord. However, beyond this, there is so much use made in the New Testament of the word day without or with different suffixes, and so much converges on those terms as a hub of consummation that there is a "day" of consummation, whether it be called "day," "day of judgment," "day of the Lord," "day of the Lord Jesus Christ," "day of Christ Jesus," "day of Christ," "day of God."[6]

II Thessalonians 2:1-3

The pretribulational contention that the "day of the Lord" includes a tribulation period prior to Christ's glorious coming is refuted by another Pauline passage. In II Thessalonians we read:

> Now we beseech you, brethren, by the coming [*parousia*] of our Lord Jesus Christ, and by our gathering together unto him, that ye be not soon shaken in mind, or be troubled, neither by spirit, nor by word, nor by

---

6. Lewis Neilson, *Waiting For His Coming*, pp. 84, 85.

letter as from us, as THAT DAY OF CHRIST is at hand. Let no man deceive you by any means: for THAT DAY SHALL NOT COME, EXCEPT THERE COME A FALLING AWAY FIRST, AND THAT MAN OF SIN BE REVEALED, THE SON OF PERDITION (II Thess. 2:1-3).

It should be pointed out that the phrase "day of Christ" employed in this passage is better rendered "day of the Lord" in this instance (R.V.). In this passage, Paul links the parousia of Christ, "our gathering together unto him," and the "day of Christ" as the same event. But this text clearly places these interrelated events after the appearance of antichrist and a time of spiritual defection, rather than before or during, as pretribulationists would contend by their designation of the terms "day of Christ" and "day of the Lord." In expounding upon this issue, LaRondelle commented:

> The efforts of dispensational writers to escape Paul's rather obvious teaching are curious. Some create an artificial distinction between "the day of Christ" (which they apply to the rapture) and "the day of the Lord" (in their view, the subsequent tribulation for Israel and the judgment of God). But how can the Day of the Lord include tribulation by the antichrist when Paul declares that the lawless one will bring his apostasy before the Day of the Lord?[7]

Paul makes it quite evident that the "day of Christ," better rendered "day of the Lord," cannot occur until these preceding events have been fulfilled—namely the apostasy and the manifestation of antichrist who will persecute the church. This does irreparable damage to the pretribulational notion that the "day of Christ" will happen before these events, or the notion that the "day of the Lord" will include them. As Gundry noted:

> It is self-evident that since these two events will occur before the day of the Lord, the day of the Lord cannot include the tribulation period during which they occur.[8]

Paul specifies that "that day of Christ" (verse 2) will transpire at Christ's parousia to gather His saints unto Himself. Paul also inserts the enlightening addition that the parousia of Christ for His saints will happen in conjunction with the destruction of the Man of sin (II Thess. 2:8).

---

7. Hans K. LaRondelle, *The Israel of God in Prophecy,* p. 202.
8. Robert H. Gundry, *The Church and the Tribulation,* p. 93.

When commenting upon the obvious truths contained within these passages from II Thessalonians, Carver added:

Here then is the plain statement of the apostle. He tells those early Christians that the proof that the Day of the Lord has not come is, not that they have not been raptured . . . BUT THAT TWO EVENTS MUST TAKE PLACE, viz. the great apostasy and the rise of the Man of Sin. Further, he cites two great events THAT ARE TO TAKE PLACE AT THE DAY OF THE LORD, viz. the Coming of the Lord Jesus, and OUR GATHERING TOGETHER UNTO HIM. Paul does not say that the Day of the Lord could not possibly have arrived because the saints are to be raptured some years earlier . . . but links the Coming of the Lord and the gathering of His People WITH the Day of the Lord in such a natural manner (there being no dispensationalists to bother about then), as to convey their complete identity. THAT IS HOW CHRISTIAN EXPOSITORS READ PAUL'S WORDS FOR 1,800 YEARS, and, unless one's mind is obsessed with 19th century theories, this is just how it reads today.[9]

The contextual placement of these Pauline points conclusively demonstrates that the parousia, "the day of Christ," "the day of the Lord," the gathering of the church unto Christ at the rapture, and the destruction of the Man of sin happen at the end of the age. They are synonymous events which will transpire simultaneously when Christ returns in glory and judgment.

I Thessalonians 5

Another key text which spells doom to the pretribulational position regarding the "day of the Lord" is located in I Thessalonians, chapter 5. It reads as follows:

For yourselves know perfectly that the DAY OF THE LORD so cometh as a thief in the night. For when they shall say, Peace and safety; then sudden destruction cometh upon them, as travail upon a woman with child; and they shall not escape. But ye, brethren, are not in darkness, that THAT DAY should overtake you as a thief (I Thess. 5:2-4).

These statements are intimately connected with Paul's information regarding the rapture of the church. Paul continues to elaborate upon

---

9. Arthur Carver, *The Great Consummation*, p. 75.

the theme of Christ's return which he had introduced in the previous chapter. He now focuses upon the constant need for spiritual vigilance and sobriety "lest that day [the day of the Lord, verse 2] should overtake you as a thief" (verse 4). He assures us that "that day" will not overtake us as the sudden intrusion of a thief providing we remain watchful and alert. It will be a day of unexpected terror for those who are asleep and drunken; but it will not be such for Christians because of our constant state of preparation, expectancy, and alertness. It will be both a day of salvation for God's people, and a day of wrath for the ungodly (verse 10).

The natural meaning of Paul's wording is that the "day of the Lord" will come upon both believers and unbelievers alike. For this reason, he continues his discussion concerning the rapture event by instructing his readers to be ready lest we be caught spiritually offguard at that day. He had not only delivered the comforting assurance regarding the blessed hope of the rapture, but he included this additional information in order to safeguard believers. He does so by providing us with the practical warning needed to insure our ultimate participation in that glorious event.

However, this point of view completely undermines the pretribulational position. They are, therefore, forced to separate the rapture removal of the church from the actual day of judgment or "day of the Lord." In spite of their attempts to lump all of the events associated with Christ's coming into the catchall interpretation of the "day of the Lord," they must ultimately distinguish between the rapture and the "day of the Lord." As Walvoord confirmed, "The Rapture is not introduced as a phase of the day of the Lord and seems to be distinguished from it."[10] They must resort to this defense or be forced to admit that Paul's warnings imply that the church will be present when the "day of the Lord" arrives like the sudden approach of a thief to unleash wrath upon the ungodly. To yield to the obvious intended application of this text would spell immediate ruin to the pretribulational contention that the church will not be present when the "day of the Lord" arrives. As Walvoord bluntly stated: ". . . the period of wrath will not overtake the church as a thief because the church will not be there."[11]

---

10. John F. Walvoord, *The Rapture Question,* p. 219.
11. Ibid., p. 221.

However, this argument amounts to nothing more than relegating Paul's warnings to absolute meaninglessness. If the rapture is to take place before the day of the Lord, then why would the apostle insist upon cautioning us to be awake "lest that day overtake (us) as a thief"? Paul's warning would be unnecessary if, as pretribulationists demand, the church will not witness the "day of the Lord." Why bother to warn believers to be watching lest that day overtake us if it will be an event which will not really come upon us at all? If the church is to be removed before the commencement of the day of the Lord, regardless of whether it follows immediately upon the heels of the pretrib rapture or seven years later, this statement would be utterly pointless.

Arguing in favor of this objection, Reese offered this conclusive observation:

> If the Day of the Lord has no reference to the Christian hope, why did the Apostle give the Thessalonians so much instruction concerning its arrival, and the necessity of sobriety and alertness on the part of Christians in view of its coming? If he held the views of pre-tribs, why did he not drop the subject of the Day of the Lord altogether when speaking to Christians, and confine himself to the Rapture? This is what pre-tribs do; they insist that Christians have not the least practical concern with the coming of the Day of the Lord as a hope, since they will have been with the Lord for years when it comes. But the awkward thing is that the Apostle, far from eschewing the giving of instruction to Christians about the Day of the Lord, has given very detailed instruction, in the Second as well as the First Epistle, about the coming of that Day; and this, not merely to arouse their interest in a subject of prophetic inquiry, but to prepare them mentally and morally for its coming. . . . If Paul believed that the Thessalonians would be raptured to heaven . . . before the Day of the Lord, what a chance he had at I Thessalonians v. 1-11 of asserting his belief! How easy to have said, "the Day of the Lord is coming, but, thank God, you will never see it, since . . . before its arrival, you will be raptured to heaven." Instead of that he has left no doubt whatever that Christians will exist on earth to see that Day; it is the day they wait for—day of joy for the redeemed, of wrath for the impenitent. . . . It is quite impossible to believe that Paul would have made these references to alertness, testing, and hope in relation to that Day, if he believed that Christains would be raptured away from the world . . . before the Day appears.[12]

---

12. Alexander Reese, *The Approaching Advent of Christ,* pp. 157, 164, 169.

II Peter 3

Another text which seriously weakens the pretribulation argument is found in II Peter, chapter three. In responding to the challenge of the last day scoffers, "where is the promise of his coming (parousia)?" (verse 4), Peter reproves them for their willful ignorance of the Noahic deluge which destroyed the antedeluvian world. He informs them that the present world is being "reserved unto fire against the day of judgment and perdition of ungodly men" (verse 7). He then continues to elaborate upon the timing of this final day of judgment by declaring:

> But the DAY OF THE LORD will come as a thief in the night; in the which the heavens shall pass away with a great noise, and the elements shall melt with fervent heat, the earth also and the works that are therein shall be burned up. Seeing then that all these things shall be dissolved, what manner of persons ought ye to be in all holy conversation and godliness. Looking for and hasting unto the COMING [*parousia*] of the DAY OF GOD, wherein the heavens being on fire shall be dissolved, and the elements shall melt with fervent heat? (II Peter 3:10-12).

In these verses, Peter directly identifies the parousia of Christ as the "day of the Lord." In Peter's understanding, they were a singular and synonymous event. He not only specifies that "the day of the Lord will come as a thief in the night" (verse 10), but indicates that it will be a time of catastrophic judgment. Nothing indicates a prolonged outpouring of wrath. The statement that "the heavens shall pass away with a great noise, and the elements shall melt with fervent heat, the earth also and the works therein shall be burned up" speaks of a sudden, decisive act of judgment. The whole passage reeks of finality and consummation.

But what is most disconcerting to the pretribulational theory regarding the "day of the Lord" is Peter's admonition to the church,

> Seeing then that all these things shall be dissolved, what manner of persons ought ye to be in all holy conversation and godliness. LOOKING FOR AND HASTING UNTO THE COMING [*parousia*] DAY OF GOD, WHEREIN THE HEAVENS BEING ON FIRE SHALL BE DISSOLVED, AND THE ELEMENTS SHALL MELT WITH FERVENT HEAT? (II Peter 3:11, 12).

It is the coming judgment by fire which provides the ground of exhortation for believers to be spiritually prepared (verse 11). However, this warning would have been completely senseless if Christians will miss the "day of the Lord." Why caution believers to be "looking for and hasting unto the coming day of God," if, according to pre-tribulational dogma, we will be raptured out of the earth before the "day of the Lord" commences? This verse clearly indicates that the "day of the Lord" coincides with the parousia of Christ, that it will happen at the day of final judgment, and that Christians are to be prepared and expectantly awaiting its arrival.

It should also be pointed out that this text harmonizes perfectly with Paul's correlative statements involving the "day of the Lord" in I Thessalonians, chapter five. Both refer to the "day of the Lord." Both texts associate it with a time of awesome judgment. And both texts insert a cautionary statement for Christians to be prepared for that approaching day. What is more, Peter concludes his statements by reminding his readers that Paul includes the same truths in his epistles (verses 15, 16). Both Peter and Paul were obviously on the same eschatological wavelength regarding the truths associated with the "day of the Lord."

These companion truths from both Peter and Paul's epistles substantiate the reality that the "day of the Lord" is the decisive, final day of judgment at the end of this age, and that Christians will live to witness it without a prior removal from the earth, as pretribulationists contend. And with these truths the New Testament is in unanimous agreement.

10

Imminency and the Early Church

Another common contention of pretribulationists is that the rapture is the next event on the prophetic calendar of events. They maintain that the rapture is imminent and, as far as they can ascertain, there are no intervening events which are prophetically scheduled to precede the coming of Christ for His saints. This belief in imminency is at the very heart of their defense and forms an essential cornerstone in the pretribulational foundation.

Imminency Defined

This concept of imminency undergirds the mainline defense of a pretrib rapture. Neilson capsulized the pretrib argument for imminency as follows:

Scripture reveals that there is to be a visible coming of Jesus Christ to earth after the destruction of Antichrist and occurrence of the great tribulation. However, Scripture also reveals that Christ on earth did not know the day nor hour of his coming and that no man knows the day or hour of his coming. This fact is made by Christ a ground of exhortation for us to watch, coupled with warnings of surprise if we do not. A seeming logical inference from such an exhortation and warning is that Christ can come at any time. If we are told to watch because we do not know the day nor hour, and to watch to avoid the possibility of being surprised by his coming, as if by a thief breaking into our house, does not that mean that Christ could come upon a person at any time? Thus the coming of Christ about which we are warned is imminent, in the sense that it can occur at any moment. By the very nature of this inference the coming about which we are warned and which is imminent must be a coming different from the coming in glory after the tribulation. For a coming that must wait the Antichrist and great tribulation is conditioned prophetically on other events, and thus cannot be imminent in the sense that it can come upon us at any moment. There must, therefore, be two comings: the rapture for the church which can occur at any time and is independent prophetically from other antecedent events, and the later coming in glory which is specifically spoken of in the Olivet Discourse and elsewhere as conditioned upon and following Antichrist and the great tribulation.[1]

This concept of imminency incorporates three essential elements: suddenness, unexpectedness or incalculability, and a possibility of occurrence at any moment.[2] Robert Gundry defined imminency as follows: "By common consent imminence means that so far as we know, no predicted event will necessarily precede the coming of Christ."[3] In keeping with the pretribulational perspective, the rapture will precede the tribulation, the great falling away, and the appearance of the Man of sin.

Pretribulationists repeatedly refer to the writings of the early church in order to bolster their position. As Walvoord confirmed, "The central feature of pretribulationism, the doctrine of imminency, is, however, a prominent feature of the doctrine of the early church."[4] They generally maintain that a pretribulation rapture can be defended on the historic grounds that it did exist, at least in incipient form, in the prophetic consciousness of the post-apostolic period. They base this argument on the inferential grounds that the early church embraced

1. Lewis Neilson, *Waiting For His Coming*, p. 154.
2. John Linton, *Will the Church Escape the Great Tribulation?* p. 12.
3. Robert Gundry, *The Church and the Tribulation*, p. 29.
4. John F. Walvoord, *The Rapture Question*, p. 51.

an "any moment" coming. In fact, when it comes to an appeal to the writings of this period, the sole shred of support for their rapture theory hangs on the slender thread of imminency. For example, while Walvoord confesses on the one hand that, "the preponderance of evidence seems to support the concept that the early church did not clearly hold to a rapture as preceding the end time tribulation period,"[5] he executes an about-face by claiming that ". . . the historical fact is that the early church fathers' view on prophecy did not correspond to what is advanced by pretribulationists today except for the one important point that both subscribe the imminency of the rapture."[6] They consistently appeal to the issue of imminency because it plays such an integral part in their prophetic system.

However, apart from a tedious review of post-apostolic literature, the early church did indeed embrace a spirit of expectancy, but they did not believe in an imminent coming of Christ before certain distinguishable events should first transpire. If any inference is to be drawn from the literature of this period, it is of a posttribulational perspective rather than an imminent pretrib rapture.

The Factor of Delay

In spite of pretribulationist appeals to the post-apostolic writings, we must determine whether the early church did, in fact, embrace a belief in an "any moment" coming of Christ. Did they believe that no distinguishable events were slated to transpire prior to the Lord's advent? Though the scriptures stress the urgent need for watchfulness and the unexpectancy in timing, they also specify or imply that certain distinct events would have to transpire first.

One of the most fundamental facts which Christ endeavored to reinforce regarding His return was the factor of delay. He repeatedly implied that there would exist a lengthy interval of time between His ascension to the Father and His return. For example, in Christ's parable of "the wise and slothful servants" He stated:

> But and if that evil servant shall say in his heart, My lord DELAYETH HIS COMING . . . (Matt. 24:48; see also Luke 12:45).

5. John F. Walvoord, *The Blessed Hope and the Tribulation,* p. 24.
6. Ibid., p. 25.

The subject of delay is also suggested in the parable of the wise and foolish virgins: "While the bridegroom TARRIED, they all slumbered and slept" (Matt. 25:5). The obvious implication of this statement is that the bridegroom's (Christ) arrival was delayed.

That a lengthy interval is implied is also brought out in the companion parables of the talents (Matt. 25:14-30; Luke 19:11-27):

> After a LONG TIME the lord of those servants cometh . . . (Matt. 25:19).
>
> . . . A certain nobleman went into a FAR COUNTRY to receive for himself a kingdom, and to return (Luke 19:12; see also Matt. 25:14 and Mark 13:34).

The phrases "after a long time," and "into a far country" correspondingly suggest that the Lord's return will be delayed.

Christ's repeated emphasis on delay was not given to undermine our need for watchful expectancy. They were given to caution the church against losing a sense of expectancy and vigilance even in the face of delay. Because of the factor of indeterminate delay, the church is admonished to maintain an attitude of readiness. Christ's exhortations to spiritual alertness are given to us not because of the guaranteed imminence of His coming, but because of the uncertainty in timing. This is demonstrated in the following passages:

> WATCH THEREFORE: FOR YE KNOW NOT WHAT HOUR YOUR LORD DOTH COME. But know this, that if the goodman of the house had known in what watch the thief would come, he would have watched, and would not have suffered his house to be broken up. THEREFORE BE YE ALSO READY: FOR IN SUCH AN HOUR AS YE THINK NOT THE SON OF MAN COMETH. Who then is a faithful and wise servant, whom his lord hath made ruler over his household, to give them meat in due season? Blessed is that servant, whom his lord when he cometh shall find so doing. Verily I say unto you, That he shall make him ruler over all his goods. But and if that evil servant shall say in his heart, My lord delayeth his coming; And shall begin to smite his fellowservants, and to eat and drink with the drunken; The lord of that servant shall come in a day when he looketh not for him, and in an hour that he is not aware of, and shall cut him asunder, and appoint him his portion with the hypocrites: there shall be weeping and gnashing of teeth (Matt. 24:42-51).
>
> Watch therefore, for ye know neither the day nor the hour wherein the Son of man cometh (Matt. 25:13).

TAKE YE HEED, WATCH AND PRAY: FOR YE KNOW NOT WHEN THE TIME IS (Mark 13:33).

And if he shall come in the second watch, or come in the third watch, and find them so, blessed are those servants. And this know, that if the goodman of the house had known what hour the thief would come, he would have watched, and not have suffered his house to be broken through. BE YE THEREFORE READY ALSO: FOR THE SON OF MAN COMETH AT AN HOUR WHEN YE THINK NOT (Luke 12:38-40).

These passages clearly indicate that the calls for alertness are not dependent so much on an imminent coming as much as they are on the uncertainty in timing. Because of the strong possibility of delay, Christians are exhorted to be prepared, watching, and alert at all seasons, lest the Lord's coming overtake us unexpectedly when we may be in a state of spiritual stupor.

It is precisely because of the uncertainty of timing that Christians are repeatedly exhorted to remain spiritually alert. The very fact that a distinct air of uncertainty constantly surrounds the actual timing of the second coming is meant to challenge Christians to ever maintain a watchful and expectant attitude lest that day overtake us suddenly, when we are unprepared. Though we will never know for certain the exact time when He will return, we can be sure that we are not caught off-guard when He comes.[7]

Furthermore, it should be stressed that none of the exhortations to watchfulness are undermined because of the factor of delay. If they did not threaten or dilute the early church's resolve to remain watchful, then they will not weaken ours either. Delay does not lessen our anticipation or expectancy. In spite of pretribulational arguments that the church cannot be genuinely motivated to watchfulness unless they believe the Lord's coming could happen any moment, reality does not support this premise. The true motivation for watching is not based on imminency, but on our ultimate accountability to Christ for the sum total of our personal conduct, heart devotion, and life style; and because of our earnest desire to be found unblameable in holiness before Him at His coming (I Thess. 3:13; see also Titus 2:12, 13 and II Peter 3:11), we endeavor to remain such.

---

7. William R. Kimball, *What the Bible Says About the Great Tribulation*, p. 212.

Imminency does not form the necessary incentive for holy living, but the ultimate recognition that our life will one day be appraised by Christ. What stimulates us to holy living should not be primarily based on an "any moment" expectancy, but on our love for Him and our sincere desire to serve him faithfully and to be found pleasing to Him. Our incentive for holiness and spiritual preparation is not jeopardized, undermined, or compromised by the factor of delay. As Allis put it: "Intensity of affection disregards time and distance . . . ."[8] The ultimate catalyst for watchfulness and preparedness draws its essential force from our earnest desire to love Christ, serve Christ, and be ready for His return, whether He returns today or tarries indefinitely.

Intervening Events?

Though the early church lived in a constant attitude of expectancy and hope for the glorious appearing of Christ, they did not anticipate Christ's return apart from the awareness that certain prophetic events would transpire first.

The issue of the Lord's imminent return had created consternation and confusion in the hearts of the Thessalonians which resulted in believers neglecting their daily responsibilities. Paul moved quickly to defuse the end time hysteria by bluntly rejecting the "any moment" theory and establishing a balanced eschatological perspective regarding the second coming. He corrected the any moment deception by reminding the Thessalonians that certain intervening events were slated to transpire first:

> Now we beseech you, brethren, by the coming of our Lord Jesus Christ, and by our gathering together unto him, that ye be not soon shaken in mind, or be troubled, neither by spirit, nor by word, nor by letter as from us, as that the day of Christ is at hand. LET NO MAN DECEIVE YOU BY ANY MEANS: FOR THAT DAY SHALL NOT COME, EXCEPT THERE COME A FALLING AWAY FIRST, AND THAT MAN OF SIN BE REVEALED, THE SON OF PERDITION (II Thess. 2:1-3).

Contrary to pretribulational assumptions, Paul categorically states that specific prophetic events will transpire before the coming of our

---

8. Oswald T. Allis, *Prophecy and the Church*, p. 169.

Lord and our gathering together unto Him. Paul flatly renounces the "any moment" theory.

> It is enough to give one pause to note Paul's indignation over this use of his name by one of the over-zealous advocates of the view that Christ was coming at once . . . . If such a "pious fraud" was so common and easily condoned as some today argue, it is difficult to explain Paul's evident anger. Moreover, Paul's words should make us hesitate to affirm that Paul definitely proclaimed the early return of Jesus. He hoped for it undoubtedly, but he did not specifically proclaim it as so many today assert and accuse him of misleading the early Christians with a false presentation.[9]

Paul cautions Christians not to be deceived, disturbed, or agitated by this imminent coming mentality. According to his information, believers were to be suspicious of any teaching which stressed that the church's gathering unto the Lord will transpire before a period of great apostasy and the manifestation of the man of sin. This fact completely undermines the contention that the early church believed in an "any moment" coming.

However, in spite of Paul's outline of events, pretribulationists consistently disregard these facts and claim that the church must, out of necessity, be removed from the earth in order for the Man of sin to be revealed. They seek to extract support for this belief from II Thessalonians 2:6, 7:

> And now ye know what withholdeth that he might be revealed in his time. For the mystery of iniquity doth already work: only he who now letteth will let, until he be taken out of the way.

They commonly infer that the "he who now letteth" and the "what witholdeth" is the Holy Spirit. They compound this speculation by assuming that since the Holy Spirit will be "taken out of the way," that this proves that the church will be raptured. As Walvoord states:

> Pretribulationists generally hold that if the Holy Spirit is removed from His present position indwelling the church, then the church itself must also be removed, and hence the rapture must take place at the same time.[10]

---

9. A. T. Robertson, *Word Pictures in the New Testament, Vol. IV,* pp. 48, 49.
10. John F. Walvoord, *The Blessed Hope and the Tribulation,* p. 127.

They further contend that the Holy Spirit in the church is exercising the restraining power which prevents the full emergence of the antichrist power, and that unless this divine deterant is withdrawn, the antichrist cannot be revealed. Though this restraining force may indeed be the Holy Spirit, there is nothing in these passages which clearly indicates this. Even if we accept that the restrainer is the Holy Spirit, there is absolutely nothing stated about the removal of the church. This premise is based upon pure conjecture.

In fact, this inference is a flagrant violation of the immediate context and a clear contradiction of Paul's statements in the same chapter. Paul nowhere indicates that the rapture is to precede the Man of sin's appearance or the falling away. If, as pretribulationists contend, the church will not be in the world when antichrist appears, then Paul's admonition to the Thessalonians that the appearance of the Man of sin and the great falling away will happen prior to the coming of the Lord and our gathering together unto Him "seems to be rather badly directed."[11] This pretrib assumption makes the orderly statements of Paul hopelessly misleading and contradictory.

According to Paul, the scriptural sequence of events should be: 1) the falling away; 2) the man of sin revealed; 3) the coming of Christ; and 4) our gathering together unto Him. But in keeping with pretribulational sentiments, the order of these events would actually be reversed. That is, 4) our gathering together unto Him (rapture); 1) the falling away; 2) the man of sin revealed; and 3) the coming of Christ (second coming). Instead of accepting the clear scriptural order of events, the pretribulational position amounts to paraphrasing II Thessalonians 2:1-3 as follows:

> Now we beseech you, brethren, concerning the coming of the Lord Jesus Christ and our gathering together unto him, that you be not soon shaken in mind, for nothing needs to happen first. That day shall come before the falling away occurs, and before the man of sin is revealed.

But contrary to this obvious contradiction of scripture, Paul specifies exactly the opposite. Whether we qualify the issue by embracing the traditional, historic perspective of interpretation which views tribulation as one of the characteristic, recurring features of the entire

---

11. George E. Ladd, *The Blessed Hope,* p. 74.

church age as opposed to an isolated period of unprecedented tribulation during the last seven years of this dispensation, or an antichrist system rather than a personalized antichrist as futurists maintain, both views are diametrically opposed to the pretribulational, "any moment" emphasis which claims that no intervening events will precede the rapture of the church, and that the church will be removed before the appearance of the Man of sin and the great falling away.

A Desperate Attempt

In recognizing the inherent danger which these verses pose for a pretrib chronology, some have attempted to minimize the impact by claiming that the "falling away" (Greek: *apostasia*) mentioned in II Thessalonians 2:3 is actually referring to the rapture. For example, E. Schuyler English[12] and Kenneth Wuest[13] have each suggested that the word "apostasia" can be interpreted, "the departure," and therefore conclude that this departure refers to the rapture. Some pretribulationists are so bent upon establishing the church's rapture removal before a final period of end time chaos and the appearance of antichrist that they strain the text by forcing it to conform to the pretrib straitjacket. This argument amounts to nothing more than unadulterated speculation.

However, this is a minority view even among pretribulationists and does not stand up to the scrutiny of scripture or the actual historical meaning and application of the word "apostasia." The word simply means "a falling away, a rebellion, or an apostasy," and the overwhelming consensus of Greek scholars confirms this definition. This forcing of scriptures amounts to little more than another desperate attempt to defend the any moment rapture theory. In commenting upon the absurdity of this example of freak exegesis, MacPherson sarcastically stated, ". . . This argument is not novel, it is nonsensical. The passage clearly refers to the apostasy—a season of falling away from faith in God."[14]

---

12. E. Schuyler English, *Re-Thinking the Rapture,* pp. 67-71.
13. Kenneth S. Wuest, *The Rapture—Precisely When?* Bibliotheca Sacra, 114:63-67.
14. Dave MacPherson, *The Incredible Cover-Up,* p. 119.

Other Objections to the "Any Moment" Theory

The "any moment" theory can also be refuted by other passages which clearly support the factor of indefinite delay or strongly imply that other intervening events must first transpire before the rapture. For example, the "Great Commission" (Matt. 28:19), which encompasses evangelism "unto the uttermost parts of the earth" (Acts 1:8), strongly suggests a long period of delay before the scope of this calling can be adequately fulfilled. As Neilson noted:

> It is true that Christ nowhere spoke in explicit fashion about the length of time until his coming, but based on his command that the gospel should be preached to the whole world . . . one could get the impression of an extended period before Christ's return. So if inferences are to be drawn, an inference of an appreciable span of history before Christ's return is not necessarily invalid.[15]

Furthermore, it should be pointed out that the "any moment theory" still faces formidable challenges in light of the present extent of worldwide evangelism and missionary outreach. Even though many claim that the world has witnessed the near completion of Christ's Great Commission to "go . . . into all the world and preach the gospel to every creature" (Mark 16:15), this widespread belief does not stand up to bibical fact or evangelistic reality.

When Jesus declared that "this gospel of the kingdom shall be preached in all the world for a witness unto all NATIONS; and then the end shall come" (Matt. 24:14; see also 28:19), He was not referring to literal nations or geographical boundaries. It is a common misconception that the word "nations" means countries, geopolitical territories, or government jurisdictions. The word nation is derived from the Greek word *ethnos* and literally means "people groups, culture groups, and tribes." According to the U.S. Center for World Missions, there are still 16,750 distinct people groups unreached by the gospel. They comprise about one-half of the world's population, or 2 billion 295 million people.

Statistics concerning the true extent of untouched people groups (*ethnos*) still remaining in the earth should sober even the most ardent defender of the "any moment theory." These statistics should also reveal the true scope of Great Commission responsibility still facing the church as it makes its steady, triumphant march of conquest unto the "uttermost parts of the earth" (Acts 1:8).

---

15. Lewis Neilson, *Waiting For His Coming*, p. 157.

But according to Christ, until the church fulfills its charge to bring the gospel to all the ethnic, people groups of the world, the end will not come. Jesus will only return for the Church when she has effectively preached the everlasting gospel "to every nation, and kindred, and tongue, and people" on earth (Rev. 14:6).

In addition, the Jewish dispersion into "all nations" (Luke 21:24) of the world following the destruction of Jerusalem in 70 A.D. also suggests a prolonged interval of time; Christ's prophecy concerning Peter's natural death (John 21:18, 19; II Peter 1:14) clearly indicates delay; Christ's repetitious statement that "I will raise him up at the last day" (John 6:39, 40, 44, 54) strongly implies that many believers will taste death before the Lord's return; the common interpretation which views the seven churches of Asia as referring to seven successive periods in church history suggests a lengthy period of time; and the parable of "the wheat and tares" (Matt. 13) implies a protracted period of time in order for both the wheat and tares to grow to maturity.

Signs, But No Signs

We might add that in spite of the "any moment" teaching which asserts that no intervening events need happen before the rapture, pretribulationists hopelessly contradict their position by claiming that the restoration of physical Israel and the re-establishment of the Jewish statehood must precede the rapture. They often appeal to the "fig tree" parable in the Mount Olivet discourse in support of this contention. They commonly refer to the "budding" of the fig tree as a prophetic proof of the restoration of Jewish statehood in 1948. For example, Lindsey affirmed that,

> . . . the most important sign in Matthew has to be the restoration of the Jews to the land in the rebirth of Israel. Even the figure of speech "fig tree" has been a historic symbol of national Israel. When the Jewish people, after nearly 2000 years of exile, under relentless persecution, became a nation again on 14 May 1948, the "fig tree" put forth its first leaves.[16]

However, the establishment of Israel's regained statehood as a precursory sign of the rapture completely shipwrecks their attempts to

---

16. Hal Lindsey, *The Late Great Planet Earth*, p. 43.

173

prove a signless, unheralded, "any moment" coming of Christ for the church.

What is more, pretribulationists are notoriously guilty of establishing a whole host of preparatory signs as clear indications of Christ's soon return. In spite of their repeated emphasis upon an imminent coming, they invariably establish a wide array of preliminary signs in order to herald the nearness of the rapture. For example, Blackstone lists seven signs.[17] Hal Lindsey lists a series of preemptive signs in his popular work entitled *The Late Great Planet Earth*.[18] Another noted pretribulationist listed ten signs.[19] And so the list goes on. But the establishment of any preliminary signs spells shipwreck for the any moment teaching. As Allis noted: ". . . The attempt to prove by signs . . . that the . . . any moment rapture must be near at hand really amounts to a surrender of the any moment principle."[20] You can't defend imminency on the one hand and establish precursory signs on the other; they are mutually incompatible. Pretribulationists' attempts to establish any signs whatsoever preceding the rapture amount to a blatant example of interpretative inconsistency which is unworthy of sound exegesis and a "rightly dividing" of God's Word. The pretribulationist "any moment theory" is one that cannot be supported by scriptural or historical fact. As Ladd concluded, "a real 'any-moment' expectation is neither Biblically nor historically sound."[21] It is a concept birthed by inference, and fostered by necessity.

---

17. William E. Blackstone, *Jesus Is Coming,* pp. 228-234.
18. Hal Lindsey, *The Late Great Planet Earth,* p. 42.
19. Clarence Larkin, *Dispensational Truth,* pp. 173-175.
20. Oswald T. Allis, *Prophecy and the Church,* p. 175.
21. George E. Ladd, *The Blessed Hope,* p. 154.

Conclusion

There is presently a widespread prophetic transformation affecting the body of Christ. This phenomenon is directly related to the renewed interest in prophetic inquiry and the re-examination of prophetic perspectives undertaken by many. In recent years, the church has witnessed increasing defections from the ranks of the pretribulational and dispensational school of prophetic interpretation. Multitudes are in the process of rejecting the pretrib position in favor of a more sensible and biblically-based perspective. Thus, many who have joined the prophetic migration have come to adopt variations of the posttribulational position. Even Walvoord, a leading contemporary proponent of a pretrib rapture, confessed that, ". . . at the present time there is a resurgence of posttribulationism."[1]

Through his extensive contacts with a diversity of Christians, MacPherson has also arrived at this significant conclusion:

---

1. John F. Walvoord, *The Rapture Question,* p. 131.

175

The pre-tribulational theory, in spite of the enormous popularity of Hal Lindsey's books, is going to continue to lose adherants. More and more Christians in America and elsewhere are taking a sober look around them—and a longer look at the New Testament. There are signs all around us that God is pouring out His Spirit on all flesh, that He is awakening His church out of her lethargy and preoccupation with fanciful speculation.[2]

Though pretribulational advocates have tended to be more vocally aggressive in their views and prolific in their writings, posttribulationism, of all persuasions, has been, and continues to be, the majority view. As Walvoord again admitted: "Posttribulationism has long been a common doctrine held by the majority of the church. . . . Posttribulationism, as far as the church as a whole is concerned, is the majority view."[3] What is particularly disturbing to pretribulationist diehards is the fact that posttribulational ranks are steadily growing.

The Confessions of Ex-Pretribulationists

Many of the scholars and laymen who cut their teeth on a pretrib diet have prophetically come of age and have gradually discarded the pretrib theory. Many individuals who have taken a sober look at the pretrib rapture teaching in the light of scipture have arrived at essentially the same conclusion as Oswald J. Smith:

Now, after years of study and prayer, I am absolutely convinced that there will be no rapture before the Tribulation. . . . I believed the other theory (pretribulationism, mine) simply because I was taught it by W. E. Blackstone in his book *Jesus Is Coming,* the Scofield Reference Bible, and Prophetic Conferences and Bible schools; but when I began to search the scriptures for myself I discovered that there is not a single verse in the Bible that upholds the pretribulation theory, but that the uniform teaching of the word of God is of a post-tribulation rapture.[4]

Smith's conclusion is particularly meaningful in light of the fact that he was such an ardent supporter of the pretribulational belief prior to his prophetic conversion. The revealing comments of other

---

2. Dave MacPherson, *The Incredible Cover-Up,* p. 149.
3. John F. Walvoord, *The Rapture Question,* p. 131.
4. Oswald J. Smith, *Tribulation or Rapture—Which?*

prominent Christian leaders who experienced a similar prophetic cross-over are indicative of the experiences of numerous Christians. This prophetic "change of mind" was humorously brought to light through the oft quoted confession of Rowland V. Bingham in his book entitled, *Matthew the Publican and His Gospel*:

> My wife set the investigating machinery going one day by saying, "Rowland, where do you get the Secret Rapture idea in the Bible? I have to teach the Second Coming to my class of young women on Sunday and I have been hunting for some proof of the Secret Rapture." I quite glibly replied, "First Thessalonians Four." "But," she said, "I have been reading that and it is about the noisiest thing in the Bible. 'The Lord shall descend from heaven with a shout, with the voice of the archangel and the trump of God . . . .'" I tried a second thrust by suggesting that there was the type of Enoch being secretly translated while Noah went through the judgment, to which there came the counter blow that knocked me out of the ring as she said, "You know, Rowland, that you cannot build a doctrine on a type." Later I said to my unsatisfied wife, "My teachers all affirmed that the Greek very clearly differentiates between the Secret Rapture of the church and the public manifestation to the world. The word parousia always indicates the rapture, while epiphaneia always has to do with the appearing of Christ with His Church . . . ." But that help-meet of mine wanted to do what I had never done, check up on these two Greek words: And so there was nothing for it but to get out my *Young's Concordance* and turn up every text in which the word parousia appeared. It smashed the theory of the Secret Rapture so hopelessly that I marveled at the credulity with which I had swallowed my "Authorities."[5]

Another who was driven to abandon his pretribulational views was Philip Mauro—one of the great Christian scholars of our century. He, like so many others initially espoused dispensational sentiments, but gradually came to recognize how scripturally anemic and ill-founded this system of interpretation really was:

> It is mortifying to remember that I not only held and taught these novelties myself, but that I even enjoyed a complacent sense of superiority because thereof, and regarded with feelings of pity and contempt those who had not received the "new light" and were unacquainted with this

---

5. Rowland V. Bingham, *Matthew the Publican and His Gospel:* cited from *Millennial Studies* by George L. Murray, pp. 137, 138.

up-to-date method of "rightly dividing the word of truth" . . . . The time came . . . when the inconsistencies and self-contradictions of the system itself, and above all, the impossibility of reconciling its main positions with the plain statement of the Word of God, became so glaringly evident that I could not do otherwise than to renounce it.[6]

In another work he added:

That system of interpretation I had accepted whole-heartedly and without the least misgivings, for the reason that it was commended by teachers deservedly honored and trusted because of their unswerving loyalty to the Word of God. But I had eventually to learn with sorrow, and to acknowledge with deep mortification, that the modern system of "dispensationalism" . . . to which I had thoroughly committed myself, not only was without scriptural foundation, but involved doctrinal errors of a serious character . . . it is common teaching nowadays (though never heard of until very recent times, so far as I am aware) that our Lord's second advent is to take place according to the following schedule: First, He will come only to the air, when the dead in Christ will rise, and they and the living saints will be caught away together, "to meet the Lord in the air" (I Thess. 4:17); and at this point the seven-year period of the great tribulation will begin. Second, at the termination of that period (some make it much longer than seven years) the Lord will resume His journey earthward, and thus complete His "coming."

The whole of this theory I am constrained to reject, because I cannot find a scrap of evidence to support it in the Scriptures; whereas there is much to be urged against it.[7]

G. Campbell Morgan, one of the most renowned of all Bible expositors, also echoed this conclusion. In an excerpt from an article in *Christianity Today.* Morgan was asked about his views regarding the validity of a pretribulation rapture in an interview with Paul G. Jackson:

(Jackson) After your long and full study and extensive exposition of the Bible, do you find any Scriptural warrant for the distinction which Bible teachers draw between the 2nd coming of the Lord "for" his own (the rapture) and the coming of the Lord "with" his own (the revelation) with a time period of 3-1/2 to 7 years between? [To this Morgan replied] Emphatically not! I know this view very well. In the earlier years

---

6. Philip Mauro, *The Gospel of the Kingdom,* pp. 6, 7.
7. Philip Mauro, *How Long to the End?* pp. 4, 15.

of my ministry I taught it and incorporated it in one of my books (*God's Method With Man*). But further study so convinced me of the error of this teaching that I actually went to the expense of buying the plates from the publisher and destroying them. The idea of a separate and secret coming of Christ is a vagary of prophetic interpretation without any Biblical basis whatsoever.[8]

Nathaniel West expressed his opposition towards the pretribulational system of interpretation with these acidic comments:

> . . . the utterly unscriptural, any-moment theory of our Lord's second coming: a theory which makes of Christ and His apostles self-contradictory teachers, and of the scriptures wholly unreliable oracles. No delusion more pleasing and sweet on the one hand, or more wild, groundless, and injurious to truth and faith, on the other, has ever captivated the minds of men, than this one of an any-moment, unseen, secret advent, resurrection, and rapture, a delusion condemned and exposed on almost every page of the Word of God.[9]

In addressing the dilemma encountered by many when re-appraising the accuracy of the pretribulation perspective, West raised this probing inquiry:

> The question is no longer a question of exegesis with such clear light before us. It is simply a question of ethics with every believer. Have we the right moral disposition toward the truth, or will we still cling to error because we have unfortunately defended it too long; shall we act against the Truth or for the Truth?[10]

This is a sobering consideration which each of us should ponder carefully.

These selected testimonies reflect the sentiments embraced by many. Multitudes have followed their lead by weaving their way through the maze of prophetic contradiction, confusion, and complexities contained within the pretribulational system. They have arrived at essentially the same conclusion—that the posttribulational persuasion is the most scripturally sound and reasonable position, and the one which shoulders the least burden of proof in seeking to establish the validity of its position.

---

8. G. Campbell Morgan, *Christianity Today,* August 1959, pp. 16, 17.

9. Nathaniel West, *The Saints Rest,* cited from *The Approaching Advent of Christ, by Alexander Reese, p. 244.*

10. Ibid., p. 244.

Through the searching of scripture, many have concluded that pretribulationism has obviously ignored the totality of scripture concerning the rapture question. It is a theory based on shallow assumptions at best, and is a scripturally destitute structure founded upon a faulty system of exegesis which is highly dependent upon inferences, conjecture, and elaborate interpretations to prop up its tenants. Many have come to the conviction that though pretribulationism appears as an impressive structure outwardly, it is, none the less, a fragile structure built upon the sands of speculation and manmade theory, rather than the reliable bedrock of scripture.

In conclusion, I should stress that questions of theology such as posttribulationism versus pretribulationism should never be decided on the basis of personal preference or prejudice. They must only be decided upon the basis of God's Word. Our biblical conclusions should never be determined by superimposing our prophetic systems upon the scriptures, or by viewing the scriptures through the tinted spectacles of prophetic bias. Instead, we must ultimately permit the Word to impose itself upon our prophetic systems, speculations, and timetables, and compel them to conform to the absolute reality of God's Word.

A Final Appeal

In closing, I recognize that the eschatological perspectives advanced within this book repeatedly challenge the prophetic opinions cherished by many; however, I do not wish to leave anyone with the subtle impression that this work is casting a negative reflection upon the integrity, sincerity, or spiritual competency of those believers who may disagree with the prophetic positions I have taken. Though I have endeavored to reasonably and scripturally enforce the prophetic viewpoints contained within this exposition, I sincerely pray that the polemic style occasionally employed has not seemed unduly abrasive. In view of the potential clash of eschatological opinions involving the material presented in this work, I earnestly appeal to each reader to thoughtfully consider the following words.

Though Christians may stand firmly together "striving for the faith of the gospel" and earnestly defending the essential tenets of the Christian faith, the speculative quality of prophetic interpretation has been, and continues to be, the grounds of contention, confusion, and dogmatism between earnest believers of differing persuasions.

Though we must be unyielding, unbending, and uncompromising concerning the essentials of our faith, we must always exercise an attitude of tolerance towards those brethren who may disagree with our prophetic positions.

The highly speculative nature of prophetic interpretation, coupled with a myriad of conflicting viewpoints, presents Christianity with a potentially volatile area of disagreement and confrontation. This potential for disagreement and discord presents a serious challenge to every believer in striving to maintain the essential balance of peace with those who may earnestly disagree with us concerning our private prophetic positions.

Our differences should never cause us to malign the sincerity or genuineness of those who do not side with our opinions. Our essential unity and fellowship in Christ should never be severed or undermined because of our differences on prophetic points. Our eschatological differences should never be made a ground of fellowship, a test of orthodoxy, or a necessary element in Christian doctrine. We must faithfully exercise the spirit of liberty and charity towards opposing viewpoints. As the old maxim goes, "In essentials unity, in nonessentials liberty, in all things charity." If we must disagree with one another in defending our prophetic opinions—we must agree to disagree—agreeably.

In the final analysis, our prophetic appraisals must always be tempered by that wisdom which is from above, which is pure, peaceable, gentle, easy to be entreated, full of mercy and good fruits, without partiality, and without hypocrisy (James 3:17). In spite of whatever divergence of opinion we may possess concerning our private prophetic positions, may we all continue striving together in the faith of the gospel, looking for, hasting unto, and loving His appearing.

Bibliography

Allis, Oswald T. *Prophecy and the Church.* Presbyterian and Reformed Pub. Co., Nutley, New Jersey, 1945.

Anderson, John A. *Heralds of the Dawn.* Author, Aberdeen, Scotland, 1946.

Bancroft, Emery H. *Christian Theology.* Zondervan, Grand Rapids, Mich., 1925.

Barnes, Albert. *Thessalonians, Timothy, Titus, and Philemon.* Baker, Grand Rapids, Mich., 1949.

_____. *Revelation.* Baker, Grand Rapids, Michigan, reprint 1983.

Bates, Leon I. *A Tribulation Map* (tract). Bible Believers Evangelistic Assoc., Sherman, Texas, 1974.

Bell, W. F. *The Errors of Dispensationalism* (tract). Free Grace Pub., Luray, Va., n.d.

Blackstone, W. E. *Jesus Is Coming.* Fleming H. Revell Co., N.Y., N.Y., 1932.

Beechick, Allen. *The Pretribulation Rapture.* Accent Books, Denver, Colorado, 1981.

Bloomfield, Arthur E. *Signs of His Coming.* Bethany Fellowship, Minneapolis, Minn., 1962.

Boatman, Russell. *What the Bible Says About the End Time.* College Press, Joplin, Mo., 1980.

Bray, John L. *The Origin of the Pre-Tribulation Rapture Teaching.* Author, Lakeland, Florida, 1982.

_____. *The Coming of Christ in I & II Thessalonians.* Author, Lakeland, Florida, 1981.

_____. *The Great Tribulation.* Author, Lakeland, Florida, 1982.

Cairns, Earle E. *Christianity Through the Centuries.* Zondervan, Grand Rapids, Mich., 1954.

Cameron, Robert. *Scriptural Truth About the Lord's Return.* Revell, N.Y., N.Y., 1922.

Carver, Arthur. *The Great Consummation.* Author, Egerton Gardens, London, n.d.

Chafer, Lewis Sperry. *Systematic Theology IV.* Dallas Seminary Press, Dallas, Texas, 1948.

Clarke, Adam. *Clarke's Commentary, Vol. 6.* Abingdon Press, Nashville, Tenn., 1833-34.

Coad, F. Roy. *A History of the Brethren Movement.* Eerdmans, Grand Rapids, Mich., 1968.

Cox, Wm. E. *Amillennialism Today.* Presbyterian & Reformed Pub. Co., Phillipsburg, N.J., 1966.

_____. *An Examination of Dispensationalism.* Presbyterian & Reformed Pub. Co., Phillipsburg, N.J., 1963.

_____. *Biblical Studies in Final Things.* Presbyterian & Reformed Pub. Co., Phillipsburg, N.J., 1968.

Dake, Finis Jennings. *Dake's Annotated Reference Bible.* Dake's Bible Sales Inc., Laurenceville, Ga., 1963.

Darby, John N. *Synopsis of the Books of the Bible, Vol. 5.* Bible Truth Pub., Addison, Ill., n.d.

Dickinson, Curtis. *Prophecy: Forbodings of the Future or Facts of the Past?* Author, Alamogordo, N.M., 1980.

Edersheim, Alfred. *The Life and Times of Jesus the Messiah.* Eerdmans, Grand Rapids, Mich., 1968.

Ewert, David: *And Then Comes the End.* Herald Press, Scottsdale, Penn., 1980.

Fields, Wilbur. *Thinking Through Thessalonians.* College Press, Joplin, Mo., 1963.

Fletcher, George B. *Predictive Prophecy* (tract). Reiner Pub., Swengel, Penn., n.d.

_____. *Will a Secret Rapture Precede the Second Coming of Christ?* (pamphlet). Chapel Library, Venice, Florida, n.d.

Froom, LeRoy E. *The Prophetic Faith of Our Fathers* (Four Volumes). Review and Herald Pub. Assoc., Washington, D.C., 1945.

Gaebelein, Frank E. *Expositor's Bible Commentary, Vol. 12.* Zondervan, Grand Rapids, Mich., 1981.

Goodwin, Lloyd L. *The Three Comings of Our Lord Jesus Christ.* Gospel Assembly Church, Des Moines, Iowa, n.d.

Grier, W. J. *The Momentous Event.* Author, The Banner of Truth Trust, Carlisle, Penn., 1945.

Guiness, H. Grattan. *The Approaching End of the Age.* Hodder & Stoughton, London, 1879.

Gundry, Robert H. *The Church and the Tribulation.* Zondervan, Grand Rapids, Mich., 1973.

Hamilton, Floyd. *The Basis of Millennial Faith.* Eerdmans, Grand Rapids, Mich., 1942.

Harrison, Everett F. et al. *Baker's Dictionary of Theology.* Baker, Grand Rapids, Mich., 1960.

Heffren, H. C. *The Sign of His Coming.* Bible Truth Depot, Swengel, Penn., 1945.

_____. *Is the Millennium Next or Never?* (tract). Bible Lovers Correspondence School, Camrose, Alberta, Canada, n.d.

Hendriksen, Wm. *Thessalonians, Timothy, and Titus.* Baker, Grand Rapids, Mich., 1977.

Henry, Matthew. *Matthew Henry's Commentary, Vol. 6.* Revell, N.Y., N.Y., 1828, 29.

Herendeen, I. C. *Is Modern Dispensationalism Scriptural?* (tract). Chapel Library, Venice, Florida, n.d.

Hoeksema, Herman. *Behold He Cometh.* Reformed Free Pub. Assoc. (Kregel),.Grand Rapids, Mich., n.d.

Ironside, H. A. *The Mysteries of God.* Loizeaux Brothers, N.Y., N.Y., 1908.

_____. *I & II Thessalonians.* Loizeaux Brothers, Neptune, N.J., 1947.

_____. *Lectures on Daniel the Prophet.* Loizeaux Brothers, Neptune, N.J., 1911.

_____. *A Historical Sketch of the Brethren Movement.* Zondervan, Grand Rapids, Mich., 1942.

Jackson, Wayne. *Premillennialism* (booklet). Author, Stockton, Ca., n.d.

Jacobson, Hezekiel; Saint, Phil. *Will Believers Go Through the Tribulation?* Christian Life Magazine, August, 1981, Vol. 43 No. 4.

Jones, Orson P. *Plain Speaking on the Rapture Question* (pamphlet). Grace Baptist Church, San Diego, Ca., n.d.

Jones, Russell B. *The Latter Days.* Baker, Grand Rapids, Mich., 1961.

Katterjohn, Arthur D. *The Tribulation People.* Creation House, Carol Stream, Ill., 1975.

Kempin, Albert J. *Why the Millennial Doctrine Is Not Biblical* (booklet). Gospel Trumpet Co., Anderson, Ind., n.d.

Kimball, Wm. R. *What the Bible Says About the Great Tribulation.* College Press, Joplin, Mo., 1983. (Also Baker, Grand Rapids, Mich., 1985.)

Kretzman, Paul E. *Popular Commentary of the Bible, Vol. 2.* Concordia Pub. House, St. Louis, Mo., n.d.

Kromminga, D. H. *The Millennium in the Church.* Eerdmans, Grand Rapids, Mich., 1945.

Lacunza, Manuel de (pen name, Juan Josafet Ben-Ezra). *The Coming of Messiah in Glory and Majesty* (translated to English by Edward Irving). A. M. London, England, 1827.

Ladd, George E. *The Blessed Hope.* Eerdmans, Grand Rapids, Mich., 1956.

LaHaye, Tim. *The Beginning of the End.* Living Books, Tyndale House Pub., Wheaton, Ill., 1981.

Larkin, Clarence. *Dispensational Truth.* Author, Philadelphia, Penn., 1918.

LaRondelle, Hans K. *The Israel of God in Prophecy.* Andrews University Press, Berrien Springs, Mich., 1983.

Leahy, Fred S. *The Roman Antichrist.* The Protestant Truth Society, London, England, 1957.

Lightfoot, J. B. *The Apostolic Fathers.* Baker, Grand Rapids, Mich., 1891.

Lindsey, Hal; Carlson, C. C. *The Late Great Planet Earth.* Zondervan, Grand Rapids, Mich., 1970.

Linton, John. *Will the Church Escape the Great Tribulation?* Author, Riverside, Ontario, Canada, 1961.

Ludwigson, Raymond. *A Survey of Bible Prophecy.* Zondervan, Grand Rapids, Mich., 1951.

MacPherson, Dave. *The Incredible Cover-Up.* Logos Int., Omega Pub., Medford, Ore., 1975.

Mauro, Philip. *How Long to the End?* Hamilton Bros., Boston, Mass., 1927.

_____. *The Gospel of the Kingdom.* Bible Truth Depot, Swengel, Penn., 1928.

McDougall, Duncan. *The Rapture of the Saints.* America's Promise Radio, Phoenix, Arizona, 1979.

McKeever, Jim. *Christians Will Go Through the Tribulation.* Omega Pub., Medford, Ore., 1978.

Morris, Leon. *The New International Commentary on the New Testament - I & II Thessalonians.* Eerdmans, Grand Rapids, Mich., 1959.

Murray, George L. *Millennial Studies.* Baker, Grand Rapids, Mich., 1948.

Murray, Iain H. *The Puritan Hope.* The Banner of Truth Trust, 1971.

Neilson, Lewis. *Waiting For His Coming.* Mack Pub. Co., Cherry Hill, N.J., 1975.

Newton, Thomas. *Dissertation on the Prophecies.* N.Y., N.Y., 1794.

Norton, Robert. *The Restoration of Apostles and Prophets, In the Catholic Apostolic Church.* T. Bosworth, London, England, 1861.

_____. *Memoirs of James and George Macdonald of Port Glasgow.* John F. Shaw, London, England, 1840.

Payne, J. Barton. *Encyclopedia of Biblical Prophecy.* Baker, Grand Rapids, Mich., 1980.

Pentecost, J. Dwight. *Things to Come.* Dunham Pub. Co. (Zondervan), Findlay, Ohio, 1958.

Peters, George N. H. *The Theocratic Kingdom* (3 volumes), Kregel, Grand Rapids, Mich., 1952.

Pierce, Robert L. *The Rapture Cult.* Signal Point Press, Signal Mt., Tenn., n.d.

Pieters, Albertus. *The Scofield Bible* (booklet). Chapel Library, Venice, Florida, n.d.

_____. *The Seed of Abraham.* Eerdmans, Grand Rapids, Mich., 1941.

Qualben, Lars P. *A History of the Christian Church.* Nelson, N.Y., N.Y., 1933.

Reese, Alexander. *The Approaching Advent of Christ.* Grand Rapids International Pub. (Kregel), Grand Rapids, Mich., 1975.

Reid, R. J. *Amillennialism.* Loizeaux Brothers, N.Y., N.Y., 1943.

Rice, John R. *Christ's Literal Reign on Earth* (booklet). Zondervan, Grand Rapids, Mich., 1939.

Riggle, H. M. *The Kingdom of God.* Faith Pub. House, Guthrie, Okla., 1899.

Robertson, A. T. *Word Pictures in the New Testament, Vol. 6.* Broadman Press, Nashville, Tenn., 1930.

Rowdon, Harold H. *The Origins of the Brethren.* Pickering and Inglis, London, England, 1967.

Bibliography

Ryrie, Charles C. *The Basis of the Premillennial Faith.* Loizeaux Brothers, Neptune, N.J., 1953.

_____. *The Ryrie Study Bible.* Moody Press, Chicago, Ill., 1976.

_____. *What You Should Know About the Rapture.* Moody Press, Chicago, Ill., 1981.

Sandeen, Ernest R. *The Roots of Fundamentalism.* The University of Chicago Press, Chicago, Ill., 1970.

Scofield, C. I. *The Scofield Reference Bible.* Oxford University Press, N.Y., N.Y., 1917.

Shepard, J. S. *The Christ of the Gospels.* Eerdmans, Grand Rapids, Mich., 1939.

Silver, Jesse F. *The Lord's Return.* Revell, N.Y., N.Y., 1914.

Sisco, Paul E. *Scofield or the Scriptures* (booklet). Chapel Library, Venice, Florida, n.d.

Smith, Oswald J. *Is the Antichrist at Hand?* Christian Alliance Pub. Co., 1927.

_____. *Prophecy - What Lies Ahead?* Marshall, Morgan, & Scott, Edinburgh, England, 1943.

Smith, Wilbur M. *Tribulation or Rapture - Which?* The Sovereign Grace Advent Testimony, London, England, n.d.

Spence, H.D.M., et al. *Pulpit Commentary* (23 Volumes). Eerdmans, Grand Rapids, Mich.

Stanton, Gerald B. *Kept From the Hour.* Zondervan, Grand Rapids, Mich., 1956.

The Researcher. *Other Certainties and Uncertainties About the Second Coming.* Fall '82, Vol. 12, No. 3. The Bible Lovers Fellowship, Sudbury, Ontario, Canada.

_____. *Who Shall Contradict the Secret Rapture Theory?* (article). Spring '83, Vol. 13, No. 1. The Bible Lovers Fellowship, Sudbury, Ontario, Canada.

The Scofield Bible, Dispensationalism, and the Conversion of the Jews (pamphlet). A Westminister Standard Pub., Gisborne, N.C., n.d.

Thiessen, Henry C. *Lectures in Systematic Theology.* Eerdmans, Grand Rapids, Mich., 1949.

Thomas, Lawrence R. *Does the Bible Teach Millennialism?* Reiner Publications, Swengel, Penn., n.d.

Travis, Stephen. *I Believe in the Second Coming of Jesus.* Eerdmans, Grand Rapids, Mich., 1982.

Tregelles, S. P. *The Hope of Christ's Second Coming.* Samuel Bagster and Sons, London, England, 1864.

Vos, Geerhardus. *The Pauline Eschatology.* Baker, Grand Rapids, Mich., 1979.

Walvoord, John F. *Armageddon.* Zondervan, Grand Rapids, Mich., 1974.

_____. *The Blessed Hope and the Tribulation.* Zondervan, Grand Rapids, Mich., 1976.

_____. *The Rapture Question.* Dunham Pub. Co. (Zondervan), Findlay, Ohio, 1957.

_____. *The Thessalonican Epistles.* Dunham Pub. Co., Findlay, Ohio, 1955.

Weeber, George G. *The Consummation of History.* Baker, Grand Rapids, Mich., n.d.

Westcott, B. F. *The Epistles of St. John.* Eerdmans, Grand Rapids, Mich., 1883.

Whitelaw, Robert L. *The Gospel Millennium and Obedience to Scripture* (booklet). The Bible Lovers Fellowship, Sudbury, Ontario, Canada, n.d.

Wilmot, John. *Inspired Principles of Prophetic Interpretation.* Reiner Pub., Swengel, Penn., 1967.

Woodrow, Ralph. *Great Prophecies of the Bible.* Author, Riverside, Ca., 1971.

_____. *His Truth Is Marching On.* Author, Riverside, Ca., 1977.

_____. *Which Year Will Christ Return?* (booklet). Author, Riverside, Ca., n.d.

Woods, Guy N. *Peter, John, and Jude.* Author, Memphis, Tenn., 1974.

Zen, Jon. *Dispensationalism* (booklet). Baptist Reformation Review, Nashville, Tenn., 1973.

Index of Scriptures